Contents

THE PERSONAL GOD

Gerald Bray

First published in 1998 by Paternoster Press

04 03 02 01 00 99 98   7 6 5 4 3 2 1

Paternoster Press is an imprint of Paternoster Publishing,
P.O. Box 300, Carlisle, Cumbria, CA3 0QS, U.K.
http://www.paternoster-publishing.com

British Library Cataloguing in Publication Data
A catalogue record for this book is available from the British Library

ISBN 0-85364-909-X

Cover Design by Forum Marketing, Newcastle upon Tyne
Typeset by WestKey Ltd., Falmouth, Cornwall
Printed in Great Britain by
Caledonian International Book Manufacturing Ltd., Glasgow

1

Introduction

Why this book has been written

This book was originally commissioned as a response to another work, *The Openness of God: A Biblical Challenge to the Traditional Understanding of God*, which was written by five North American professors of theology in 1994.[1] It was published by Inter-Varsity Press in the United States and by Paternoster Publishing Company in the United Kingdom and received wide publicity at the time because of its untraditional approach to the Christian doctrine of God. Following a number of critical reviews,[2] the British publishers decided to publish a response to it and asked me if I would undertake that task. No conditions were placed on this invitation other than that the book should be short (about 25,000 words) and produced quickly enough to reach the public before *The Openness of God* disappeared from view. However, it would be fair to say that the general understanding

---

[1] Clark Pinnock (McMaster Divinity College, Hamilton, Ontario), Richard Rice (La Sierra University, Riverside, California), John Sanders (Oak Hills Bible College, Bemidji, Minnesota), William Hasker (Huntington College, Huntington, Indiana) and David Basinger (Roberts Wesleyan College, Rochester, New York).
[2] See especially those by Roger Olson, Douglas Kelly, Timothy George and Alister McGrath, published together in *Christianity Today* on 9 January 1995, and the one by Frederick Leahy in the April 1997 issue of *Evangelicals Now*.

was that my response would come from a traditional standpoint and be acceptable to those who criticized the radicalism of the original work. Books, however, tend to have a life of their own, and no doubt many who read this will never have seen *The Openness of God*. One thinks, for example, of J. I. Packer's well-known *Fundamentalism and the Word of God*, which was originally written in response to Gabriel Hebert's *Fundamentalism and the Church of God*, which had in turn been inspired by Billy Graham's mission to London in 1954 and which is now all but forgotten. Packer's book, on the other hand, is still in print and there must be many thousands who have read it and know no more of Hebert's text than what they have found there.

I cannot pretend that *The Personal God* will have a similar future, but I have felt it important to bear in mind the needs of readers who, although they may be concerned with the fundamental issues at stake, are unfamiliar with the immediate cause of the book's composition and will not read the work it was intended as a response to. Reviews of *The Openness of God* have taken up particular details in it which have been the cause of controversy and concern. This book will also deal with these points, but within a more general framework. It is not intended to be a direct critique of *The Openness of God* in the way that a book review would be.

In order to do justice to my commission from the publisher, I have taken the following approach. First, I have tried to understand what it is that the theologians who wrote *The Openness of God* are trying to communicate to the Christian public, and particularly to the evangelical wing of the church, to whom the book is specifically addressed. I have then gone on to outline what I see as the essential framework for any doctrine of God, whether it is 'evangelical' or not. Readers will of course notice that the author is writing from that standpoint, but the questions raised and the answers proposed take us beyond the parameters of any one branch of Christianity and reach out to embrace the whole. Traditional Christians who are Roman Catholic, Eastern Orthodox or non-evangelical Protestants might wish to phrase some things differently, but I hope that in the pages which follow they will all recognize the common faith which we share. At the same time, I hope that non-traditional readers, while they will no doubt disagree with many of the things expressed here, will nevertheless see that this is not simply a reiteration of a standard line which they have rejected, but an attempt to restate the faith once delivered to the saints in a way which addresses their concerns with the seriousness they deserve.

To state the problem briefly, the authors of *The Openness of God*, in common with many modern theologians, are unhappy with what they regard as the 'traditional doctrine of God'. Of course it is possible to quarrel with their definition of this, and even to question whether what is commonly known as 'classical theism' is really what most Christian writers through the ages have thought and taught. It is particularly worrying to note that what they appear to be doing in fact is writing a critique of the Puritan divine Stephen Charnock (1628–80).[3] It is no criticism of him to say that his book provides a very slender base as the chief source for the 'traditional doctrine', and one which has never carried any official weight in the church. Other traditional writers may or may not agree with what Charnock says, but very few of them would have taken his views into account when writing, and there is no school of Charnock in the sense that there are schools of Aquinas, Luther and Calvin. It would have been better if the authors of *The Openness of God* had chosen a more representative source for their assertions of what the traditional doctrine is,[4] though of course there can be no doubt that Charnock was trying to defend his understanding of it.

The authors of *The Openness of God* also belong to a type of Protestantism which not only rejects the authority of the church's tradition, but sets it up in contrast to the teaching of Scripture. At times it seems that in their minds the Bible stands in sharp conflict with the history of Christian theology, even

---

[3] *Discourses upon the Existence and Attributes of God* (reprint, Grand Rapids, 1979).

[4] In such matters it is usually best to take some ecclesiastical confession of faith, such as the Westminster Confession of 1647, rather than the writings of any one individual.

though all genuinely Christian theologians have regarded the right interpretation of Scriptural doctrine as their primary task. Perhaps they did get some things wrong, and of course none of us is perfect, but it is hard to believe that in the late twentieth century a few radicals have arrived at a truth which has escaped generations of sincere searchers. It may well be that the modern age is asking different questions, which must be addressed in a fresh way, but that is not in itself sufficient ground for denying the validity of the inherited tradition. It is at least possible that what theologians of an earlier time were trying to express can be restated in such a way as to meet modern concerns, without calling their faithfulness to Scripture into question.

The authors of *The Openness of God* are rightly concerned to avoid a method of reading the Bible which is normally called 'proof-texting'. This involves taking verses at random, out of context, and using them to support whatever it is that one wishes to say. They accuse the classical tradition of citing an almost endless number of biblical texts in support of a doctrine of God which is fundamentally unbiblical because it neglects the underlying spirit and direction of Scripture. Of course, it is always possible to do this, as the fourth-century Arians demonstrated. By assembling a wide range of Bible verses taken out of context, they were able to 'prove' that the Scriptures taught that the Son of God was a creature, inferior to the Father, who alone was truly God. But those who criticize such an approach have to show that what they are proposing is really more faithful to the inner meaning of the Bible than what they are attacking, and it is more than doubtful whether the authors of *The Openness of God* have succeeded in doing this.

Such a demonstration would require a much more extensive treatment of the subject than they have given it, but even if we accept this limitation, there are problems with the method they adopt and the conclusions which they come to which must make us pause. As they quite rightly recognize, being 'biblical' is not as easy as it sounds, and those who try to achieve this aim without taking the church's theological tradition into account may well end up with a pattern of belief which is less profound and less consistent than the one which they are attacking. What has been painstakingly pieced together over centuries may indeed fall to pieces if it is criticized in the right way, and there are some scientific discoveries (like Einstein's theory of relativity) which can be cited to prove this point. But this does not happen every day, and when it does, it requires the most careful and complete analysis, which a book the size of *The Openness of God* obviously cannot provide. In this case, there is good reason to believe that even a more thorough treatment of the question will not yield such a result because the fundamental criticism which they are making is misplaced to begin with. That, at least, is what this book will try to argue.

The objection to classical theism and the proposed alternative

Before we can begin to respond, it is important that we try to examine the motives for the criticism of traditional theism in this book. In controversies of this kind, it often appears that what the protagonists are trying to affirm has a certain validity, but that problems arise when we look at what they feel compelled to reject or deny in the process. Unfortunately, it is all too easy to look at a book like *The Openness of God*, criticize it for what it rejects, and then conclude (unfairly) that it has nothing valuable or important to say. Such an approach will not persuade the authors of anything other than the obtuseness of the defenders of traditional theism – something which they seem to assume! It might even provoke a counterblast which would miss the point of the original criticism and lead to a dialogue of the deaf, which is unfortunately all too common in theological circles. It is therefore important to present their case in as positive a light as possible before attempting to provide an alternative response to it. Such a response must be more than just a rebuttal of their views. It must also attempt to integrate their concerns into a framework which, while compatible with traditional positions, makes a serious effort to deal with the issues which made them ask questions in the first place.

What the authors of *The Openness of God* are trying to affirm is that our God is a God who answers prayer. He is not a remote deity who is so different from us that he cannot comprehend our needs and requests. Nor is his plan for the world so predetermined that he cannot respond to us unless we happen to ask for something which is already part of his plan (in which case prayer is really superfluous). They attack traditional theism because it portrays a God who is *immutable*, a concept which they take to mean that he never changes in any way at all, and is therefore unable to respond in any real way to prayer. They think that such a doctrine is incompatible with a living relationship between God and people who live in a world of time and space and who are changing all the time. If God cannot adjust to this, their argument runs, he cannot relate to us. But the Bible clearly portrays a God who does relate to us, who hears our prayers, and who takes care of his people. Therefore we must conclude that divine immutability is an untenable concept, and much the same might be said of the rest of the classical package, though this is implied rather than clearly stated or argued.

According to the authors of *The Openness of God*, what makes God tick is *love*, the quality which defines his essence. Love implies relationship, which in turn implies mutability, since all relationships grow and change over time. Therefore, if we are to maintain the biblical doctrine that 'God is love' (1 John 4:15), we have little choice but to reject classical theism. At this point one might well ask how the church could have been so terribly wrong for such a long time. The answer is provided by appealing to the nefarious influence of 'Greek philosophy', especially Platonism, which is supposed to have dominated the thinking of the church fathers. Through them, ideas derived from Platonism came to be accepted as the basic framework for doing Christian theology, and have remained so ever since. This influence may have been challenged at certain times (notably in the sixteenth-century Reformation) but it has never been shaken off. On the contrary, after an initial protest, the Reformers went back to the scholasticism which they had theoretically rejected and produced a Protestant version of it. This is where Stephen Charnock comes in, and all subsequent defenders of the Puritan heritage may be tarred with the same brush.

In fairness, it should be said that the gist of the above argument was not invented by the authors of *The Openness of God*, nor is it a product of the most recent modern theology. It originated in the early nineteenth century in Germany, where it was connected with such names as Ferdinand Christian Baur (1792–1860) and August Neander (1789–1850). Later on, it was picked up by Albrecht Ritschl (1822–89), but the classic exposition which became famous all over the world is that of Alfred von Harnack (1851–1930), expressed most clearly in a series of lectures delivered in Berlin in 1900 and published in English translation as *What is Christianity?*[5] Harnack's thesis was later developed further by Walter Bauer (1877–1960)[6] and has gained wide acceptance, even though it has been refuted in considerable detail by such eminent scholars as J. N. D. Kelly (1909–97)[7] and H. E. W. Turner (1907–95)[8] and is no longer taken seriously by church historians. It comes as a surprise to see this old idea served up as something new, but these things take time to percolate across disciplines, and perhaps this is the way it appears to people who have been trained in systematic theology at conservative institutions where Harnack and Bauer would not have been studied. More alarmingly though, the authors of *The Openness of God* show no sign that they have discovered where this idea comes from, nor do they appear to be aware that it has been convincingly refuted by the above-named scholars among others. This is a serious weakness in their argument, which will have to be considered in due course.

Finally, it can be said in their favour that the authors of *The Openness of God* are concerned to root their theology in the devotional life of the individual believer. This desire to be

---

[5] The German title was *Das Wesen des Christentums*.
[6] *Orthodoxy and Heresy in Earliest Christianity* (London, 1972). The book was originally published in German in 1934.
[7] See especially his *Early Christian Creeds*.
[8] In *The Pattern of Christian Truth* (London, 1954).

practical is obviously a good thing, and if traditional theology really is remote from everyday spirituality, then it can rightly be criticized. How far this is true, and whether it can be put down to problems of expression rather than to matters of substance, is unclear, but if there is such a gap then those who wish to defend it must address the situation and overcome it. Most observers of the evangelical scene (in particular) would probably agree that there is a gap of some kind, though they may define it in different ways. Broadly speaking, it seems that on the one side we have the intellectuals, Calvinists and academic theologians, who go on speaking a language rooted in seventeenth-century concepts, while on the other side are the charismatics, Arminians and evangelists, many of whom are prominent church leaders even if they would not normally be called theologians. In sharp contrast to the former, they speak the language of today and use it to convey quite a different message.

The authors of *The Openness of God* appear to be men who were brought up in the first of these worlds, who have seen that it does not speak to the second (where the action is), and who have felt it to be their duty to cross over the divide and provide a viable theology for those who live life 'where it's at'. Perhaps they have been unfair to those whom they criticize, and it may well be that those who are 'where it's at' are not listening to them, but if there is any truth in this analysis, then it is a serious problem which must be squarely faced. To that extent at least, the authors of *The Openness of God* are right to say that repeating traditional formulas is not enough, and that a new approach is needed. Whether that new approach should involve a change of fundamental doctrine though is another matter, and it is this issue which will have to be addressed in the pages which follow as we think about how to express the biblical understanding of God.

2

The God of the Bible

Creation and providence

Before we get into systematic theology it is probably a good idea to take a quick look at the way God appears as an actor in the biblical drama. Of course, this cannot be crudely separated from systematic theology, which takes the biblical data as its foundation, but what we have in mind here is the way God acts in the broad sweep of biblical history. This is how his revelation unfolds in practice. Systematic theology is the theory which attempts to explain that practice, but it can never take its place. The faithful preacher and teacher of God's Word must understand the basic principles of systematic theology, but he must also be able to convey them through the historical form in which that Word has been given to us.

'In the beginning, God created the heavens and the earth' (Genesis 1:1). This simple statement sets the stage for everything which follows, and is fundamental to our understanding of God. He is the creator of everything that exists. Today this statement sounds unexceptionable to most of us, but in the early days of Christianity there were a lot of people who found it impossible to accept. Oddly enough, their basic concern was remarkably similar to that of the authors of *The Openness of God*. They could not believe that the God whom Jesus called his Father was also the creator of a world which is full of suffering and evil. Why would such a good and loving God make a universe like this one? But rather than conclude that God is part of his suffering world, they took the opposite path and declared that he was not responsible for it at all. Instead there was another god, the so-called 'demiurge' ('creator'), who was a being inferior to the true God and unworthy of our worship.

Christians responded to this suggestion by saying that according to Genesis God created everything. Moreover, when he had finished 'he saw that it was good'. In other words, the world is not evil in itself. It is an orderly universe, in which things happen regularly according to natural ('scientific') laws. They did not fully understand those laws – and even after many years of thrilling discoveries, there is still an enormous amount which we do not know about them – but they knew that they were there and that they could not be broken. But these Christians were not deists, that is to say, they were not people who believed in a clockwork universe which God may have created but over which he exercises no ongoing control. The unbreakable laws of nature could be suspended or transcended when God so desired, and there were various occasions when he did just that. The results were what we call 'miracles', of which the greatest by far were the virginal conception of Jesus and his later resurrection from the dead.

Sometimes, the early Christians admitted, a miracle might also have a 'natural' explanation, as for example when the River Jordan was stopped to let the children of Israel walk across its bed. It was possible that this was the result of a minor earthquake (or something similar) which temporarily blocked the stream. But even if such explanations could sometimes be found, the events were still miracles because of their timing. The biblical writers never stopped to speculate about the mechanics of what happened; to them the important thing was that the event occurred *when* it did, with the results which are recorded for us in the Bible. Then, as now, timing was everything.

The existence of evil in a world created and governed by a good God is a problem which the Bible never explains, and which nobody has ever resolved to general satisfaction. It remains a mystery, but both the biblical writers and the early Christians regarded it as a fact which we all have to reckon with. They were less concerned about explaining how it occurred than they were about explaining what to do about it. What the Bible does do, however, is say that evil in the world is the result of *disobedience* to the commands of God. Such disobedience is only possible in creatures who have free will, of which there are two types. The first are the angels, of whom a number revolted against God and fell, along with their leader Satan (also called Lucifer or the devil). Satan then enticed the second type of creature who possessed free will – human beings – and they succumbed to his temptation. As a result, they also fell, and are now in spiritual subjection to the devil who tricked them.

Because of all this, there is now no human being who is not subject to this curse. It does not matter whether we have done anything 'bad' or not; we are sinners by birth and by inheritance from our first parents. This is a hard teaching for many people to accept, but its truth is borne out by experience. Even a newborn baby is selfish by nature, and every parent knows that to spare the rod is to spoil the child – there is no such thing as infant innocence. It is certainly true that every human society has learned to control this evil within by developing elaborate codes of behaviour and laws which are designed both to restrain what is negative and encourage what is positive in human life, but this does not take the problem away. When these codes break down, as they do from time to time, the evil inside us resurfaces and wreaks havoc until it is put back under control.

It used to be thought that as human society evolved, so the propensity towards evil would be overcome. Evil was thought to be the result of circumstances, and it was hoped that improving these would lead to a cure. Experience has shown that this is true in a sense, because as social conditions are bettered, certain types of wrongdoing are reduced. When there is full employment, for example, the tendency to indulge in petty crime is lessened because there is neither the need nor the time for it. But that is not at all the same thing as saying that evil itself can be eradicated by such means. Our own time has demonstrated that those who control the levers of power in the most developed societies possess a potential for evil of which their forefathers could only dream. As a result, mass destruction has become a phenomenon which continues to plague the twentieth century long after the horrors of Hitler and Stalin have passed into history. Around the world, in places like Rwanda, the Sudan and Bosnia, thousands and even millions of people have been killed in the past ten years, and there seems to be no effective way of stopping the killing. Instead, more and more people are being numbed into acquiescence as the toll of deaths passes human understanding. Add to this the unrelated, but still very great number of deaths resulting from abortion, preventable disease and so on, and the figures climb even higher.

The Bible says that all this is to be expected, because the root of evil does not lie in the world but in the heart of individual people who have rebelled against God. No matter what social arrangements we make, there will be wars and rumours of wars until the end of time. Poverty and disease may change their shape, but they will never be eradicated. Hatred, envy, malice and the like will continue to exist, because these things are unaffected by economic indicators. The only hope we have is that God himself will intervene to save us, and this is what most of the Bible is about.

God's plan of salvation begins with Noah. In the story of the great flood, the whole of humanity is destroyed, apart from a remnant which is saved in the ark. After the waters subside, that remnant is allowed to resume its life on earth, and God promises Noah that never again will he destroy the world because of human sin. In spite of the continuing existence of evil, the earth will be preserved until there is a final consummation, when judgment will be given and evil will receive its just deserts. Like it or not, this is the world we live in – a flawed creation in which God's designs have to be understood against the background of preservation from evil which the covenant made with Noah talks about.

The picture of God which emerges from this is one of a sovereign deity who is in control of events, but who has permitted rebellion against his declared purposes to exist and even to flourish 'as long as the earth endures' (Gen. 8:22). But in spite of this toleration of evil, justice will be done in the end. When that great and terrible day comes, only the righteous, who have done God's will as he has revealed it to them, will be saved from the final judgment and the eternal punishment which will follow.

Now there can be no denying that this picture of God and his justice has caused a lot of problems, not least among those righteous people who have had to suffer the consequences of God's decision to permit the continuing existence of evil. The Old Testament is full of examples of God-fearing men and women who have questioned God's patience in this matter, even to the point of losing their faith. Psalm 73, traditionally ascribed to Asaph, puts it very well:

> But as for me, my feet had almost slipped; I had nearly lost my foothold.
> For I envied the arrogant when I saw the prosperity of the wicked.
> They have no struggles; their bodies are healthy and strong.
> They are free from the burdens common to man; they are not plagued by human ills . . .
> From their callous hearts comes iniquity; the evil conceits of their minds know no limits . . .
> They say: 'How can God know? Does the Most High have knowledge?' . . .
> Surely in vain have I kept my heart pure; in vain have I washed my hands in innocence.
> All day long I have been plagued; I have been punished every morning.
> If I had said: 'I will speak thus', I would have betrayed this generation of your children.
> When I tried to understand all this, it was oppressive to me,
> till I entered the sanctuary of God; then I understood their final destiny.
> Surely you place them on slippery ground; you cast them down to ruin.
> How suddenly are they destroyed, completely swept away by terrors!
> (2–5; 7; 11; 13–19).

It has to be admitted that Asaph's answer does not satisfy everybody, for the simple reason that it appears to be so obviously unfair. If someone has done wrong he should be punished for it, and not allowed to continue. That is the way that human justice works (or tries to), and it seems both wrong and illogical that divine justice, if there is any, should be different. If anything, people argue, God's retribution should be quicker and more complete than that of a human tribunal. Why does the opposite appear to be the case? The Bible does not answer this question directly, as the verses of the psalm indicate. Instead, the doubter is challenged by something quite different – the way to resolve these dilemmas, says the psalmist, is to turn to God and look for comfort in a closer relationship with him.

This brings us to the question of *faith*, for which we have to go back to the covenant which God made, not with Noah but with Abraham and his descendants. Faith is the context in which the answer to the problem of evil must be found. It is a practical solution to the problem, not a theoretical one. At the theoretical level, no answer is given to us, nor will there be in this life. But in practical terms, we are provided with a key which will help us to overcome the difficulty and to deal with issues as they arise, even if we cannot fully explain them.

The covenant of grace and faith

In Genesis 12 we are told that God called Abraham,[9] a man who lived in what is now Iraq, to leave his home and travel far to the west where he would find a land in which his family would settle and prosper. Abraham was childless, he had presumably never gone very far from home before, and he had no idea what reception might await him, but in spite of all that he got up and went. With little or no evidence to go on, he believed the voice of God speaking to him and he was rewarded accordingly. His previously barren wife conceived a son, he settled in the land of Canaan, which is now Israel (or Palestine) and he lived long enough to see the beginnings of the fulfilment of God's promises to him. What motivated Abraham was *faith* – a trusting response to God's call. But this faith would not have been possible if God had not revealed himself to

---

[9] He was actually called Abram at first, but for the sake of clarity and simplicity I have stuck to the more familiar name throughout.

Abraham to begin with. Why this happened in the way that it did is a mystery which has never been explained. Its strangeness is well summed up in the popular rhyme:

> How odd
> of God
> to choose
> the Jews.

This 'oddity' on God's part was noted by the Israelites themselves, who realized that in human terms there was little reason for God to have chosen them. This is quite clearly stated in Deuteronomy 7:7–9:

> The Lord did not set his affection on you and choose you because you were more numerous than other peoples, for you were the fewest of all peoples. But it was because the Lord loved you and kept the oath which he swore to your forefathers that he brought you out with a mighty hand and redeemed you from the land of slavery, from the power of Pharaoh king of Egypt. Know therefore that the Lord your God is God; he is the faithful God, keeping his covenant of love to a thousand generations of those who love him and keep his commands.

Interestingly enough, in the early days of the Christian church, the Apostle Paul said much the same thing to the Corinthians (1 Cor. 1:26–29):

> Brothers, think of what you were when you were called. Not many of you were wise by human standards; not many were influential; not many were of noble birth. But God chose the foolish things of the world to shame the wise; God chose the weak things of the world to shame the strong. He chose the lowly things of this world and the despised things – and the things that are not – to nullify the things that are, so that no one may boast before him.

From this we learn that God's covenant relationship with his people is one of *grace*; in other words, it is based on his free favour

and choice. Even if there is a sense in which it is true that we are
called to respond to him, this can only happen because of his prior
decision to speak to us and the power which he gives us to answer
him. Furthermore, we learn that although God's covenant promises are unchanging and unchangeable, their fulfilment is not
necessarily straightforward. If the covenant promises are to be
realized, they must be received in obedience, and obedience does
not come naturally to a race which is in rebellion against its
creator. For this reason, it too must be a gift of God. Without that,
our response can only be negative, which is why it is impossible
to make an independent choice to believe in God. All we can do
'independently' is to continue in unbelief, which is what we have
inherited from our first parents.

The development of the covenant

The covenant made with Abraham remains fundamental to both
Judaism and Christianity, but the story does not end there. That
covenant was renewed with Isaac and Jacob, and then (in a rather
different way) with Moses. Theologically speaking, we can as-
similate Isaac and Jacob to Abraham, but Moses demands special
treatment. There are two incidents in his life which are particularly important for our present purposes. The first is his meeting
with God in Exodus 3, and the second is the giving of the law in
Exodus 20. On the first occasion, God appears to Moses in a
burning bush and tells him two things. The first is that he reveals
his name – I AM, which was subsequently transformed into the
Hebrew word *YHWH*.[10] God then says that he is the God of
Moses' ancestors, mentioning Abraham, Isaac and Jacob, indicat-
ing that what might appear to be a new departure is really a
continuation of the covenant he had made with them. The precise
nature of this renewal becomes clear later on, when Moses

---

[10] Normally pronounced 'Yahweh', but we cannot be sure because
written Hebrew has no vowels and the name of God was never spoken
aloud. See the next chapter for a full discussion of this.

receives the law 'written by the finger of God' (Ex. 31:18). In the law, God outlines how the covenant is to be observed in detail. What we learn from this is that Israel is to be a nation set apart, or made 'holy' to God. Holiness is revealed as something fundamental to God's character, and what is more, it is something which his covenant people are able to share in some mysterious manner.

This does not mean that the people are called to become like God as he is in his own being. The ways in which they were to manifest their holiness were tailored to meet their situation, and could not be applied to God himself. After all, what would it mean to say that God committed himself to avoiding certain types of food? The essence of holiness cannot therefore lie in commands like these, but must be sought somewhere else altogether. The link between Israel and God was essentially a spiritual one, even if this was often lost sight of. In writing to the Romans about it, the Apostle Paul makes this point quite clearly, and berates the Jews of his time for relying on the externals of the law as signs of their holiness, and ignoring any serious heart and life commitment to the covenant. Similar situations have occurred often enough in Christian circles for us to be able to believe that this is an endemic problem. Only people who are spiritually minded themselves can understand the true meaning of God's commands and promises. Those who lack this awareness will inevitably be reduced to external observances, and in the process these will bring them into disrepute because they will no longer be used in the way which was originally intended.

The Mosaic renewal of the covenant is the first time that human beings are told specifically both who God is and what he is like. Furthermore, they are told these things not in order to emphasize the vast gulf which separates them from God, but in order to give them a way in which they can overcome that distance and relate more closely to him. Knowing God's name puts the people on more intimate terms with him than they were before, and being given guidance on becoming holy allows them to imitate something of his character. In this way they are given the means to become more like him, but there is a price to pay. Greater privileges mean greater responsibility, and it was here that Israel was to fail so dramatically in the years ahead. In the words of the Apostle Paul: 'When the commandment came, sin sprang to life and I died.' (Rom. 7:9). What was true of him as an individual was true of the nation as a whole, as the story in Exodus goes on to make perfectly clear.

Even when Moses was up the mountain getting the law, the people who were supposed to receive it were making a golden calf to worship (Ex. 32). God immediately realized just how unworthy they were, and wanted to abandon them altogether, but Moses intervened on Israel's behalf, reminding God of his promises and of what he had done for them already. Surely, Moses pleaded, God would not abandon his purposes now? In response to this plea, God agreed to maintain the covenant, because he accepted the validity of what Moses was saying and respected his faith in the covenant promises. This incident is a classic case where people like the authors of *The Openness of God* claim that the Lord changed his mind in answer to a human prayer. Is this right?

To say that God 'changed his mind' (cf. Ex. 32:14) may make some sense from Moses' standpoint, but it is only superficially true, because God's true intentions remained the same after this incident as they had been before. The threat of annihilation was certainly a real one, and it reflects what God will do to unrepentant sinners on the day of judgment. It serves as a reminder that we cannot presume on God's promises if we persist in disobeying his commandments. But at the same time, it has to be read in the context of the relationship which God had established with Moses as the leader of his people. What kind of leader would Moses have been if he had agreed with God's assessment and gone off on his own, to found a new covenant nation? Do we want the captain to desert the ship when the going gets tough? Hardly. God had to teach Moses his responsibility, and remind him that leading Israel was not going to be an easy matter. The story shows that Moses was the right man to have chosen, because in spite of everything, his love for the people was greater than his disgust at their actions. It also shows what the relationship between Moses and God was based on – faith, the bond which holds it all together and ultimately makes the fulfilment of the promises possible.

As far as Israel is concerned, the meaning here may be summed up in the famous words of Jesus: 'Many are called but few are chosen' (Matt. 20:16). It was true that Israel as a nation had received the calling of God, but this did not mean that every Israelite would automatically be saved. As subsequent events were to show, only a minority of Israelites would persevere to the end, a sad fact which was duly noted by the prophet Isaiah, who exclaimed (Isa. 1:9):

> Unless the Lord Almighty had left us some survivors, we would have become like Sodom, we would have been like Gomorrah.

By the time the history of the Old Testament drew to a close, Israel had lost ten of its twelve tribes, its sacred monarchy and its national independence. But in the process, its worship of God had been purified of alien accretions and its sense of destiny as the Lord's chosen people had been reinforced. In spite of all its trials, Israel was arguably closer to God at the end of the Old Testament period than it had been at the beginning. Certainly it would never again fall prey to syncretistic polytheism and so find itself being assimilated into the surrounding nations. Individual Jews might – and did – cross over to the Gentiles, but the nation as a whole maintained its particular religious identity against all odds.

The second renewal of the covenant took place in the time of King David, who was promised that his dynasty would rule over the nation for ever. What did this mean? In purely historical terms, 'for ever' lasted about 400 years, until the destruction of Jerusalem in 586 BC and the captivity of the people in Babylon. It looked to many people as if God's promise had failed, but in reality it was to be fulfilled at a higher level – in the person and work of Jesus Christ, descended from David according to the flesh and the ultimate inheritor of all the promises first made to him, but also the Son of God and the founder of a new and spiritual kingdom which was both in history and beyond it.

This stage of covenant renewal teaches us two things. First, we learn that God is going to get more deeply involved with the human race than he has ever been before. David and, even more, his son Solomon represent this in their lives and accomplishments. The founding of Jerusalem and the building of the temple as the place where God's holy name is placed are moments of covenant fulfilment which were not to be surpassed until the one who was greater even than Solomon should appear. Now God was going to be present among his people, though without ceasing to be the Lord of the universe at the same time. The Israelites did not stop to think that this involved some kind of philosophical contradiction, nor did they presume to adopt a degree of familiarity with God which would diminish his divine majesty and 'otherness'. To them, it was a blessing to be received with gratitude and accepted as the great privilege that it was. The balance between a sense of God's presence and his continuing distance was to remain characteristic of temple worship as long as that continued.

Second, we learn from the covenant renewal under David and Solomon that God's promises are essentially spiritual in nature. His kingdom is not of this world, and his purposes for his people are rooted in another dimension of reality altogether. This does not mean that we are to despise the present world, or regard it as irretrievably lost and hostile to God, but neither are we to think of it as the ultimate reality and put all our hopes in it. It is a place of preparation for something better, which God has willed for us. We see him at work 'through a glass darkly' (1 Cor. 13:12, AV) and are unable to understand everything that happens, but at the same time we have a relationship with God which gives us the faith to believe that he has a purpose for us, as well as the hope that one day we shall understand why that purpose has been worked out in the way that it has.

Jesus and the renewal of the covenant

When we turn to the New Testament, we find that we are in a new situation in which God is doing something he has never done before. His covenant relationship with Israel was already well established and his revelation to the Israelites was known, but there was still something missing. Many Jews sensed this and were waiting eagerly for the coming of the Messiah, or 'anointed one'[11] who would rescue them from their troubles and fulfil the promises made to Abraham, Moses and David. The New Testament message is that this hope was realized in the life, death and resurrection of Jesus of Nazareth. But the nature of God's work in Jesus is quite different from anything which had gone before, and this difference is clearly symbolized right at the beginning – in his birth. It was not unusual for extraordinary births to occur as portents of God's intentions and there are several examples of this throughout the history of Israel. Isaac, Samson, Samuel and even John the Baptist all came into the world by supernatural means. But in each of their cases, the pattern was that God spoke to a woman who was too old to conceive a child, and then her barren womb was opened. In the case of Jesus, however, divine intervention worked in exactly the opposite way. Far from performing a miracle which everyone would immediately recognize as such, God chose to speak to a young girl who had probably just reached puberty, and told her that she would have a child without sexual intercourse.

This story has become so hallowed by centuries of devotion that it is hard for us to imagine how it must have sounded to those who first heard it. Unmarried girls get pregnant all the time, but nobody thinks that this is the result of divine intervention. People in those days were equally sceptical, and when Joseph (Mary's fiancé) heard about it he decided not to marry her (Matt. 1:19). But God spoke to him too, and told him that what Mary was saying was true – she had conceived a child by the Holy Spirit. This child was not only going to be an extraordinary man, along the lines of the Old Testament figures just mentioned; he was also going to be God in human flesh – a totally new departure in the ongoing process of God's self-revelation to us.

Of course, many people are ready to believe that the life and teachings of Jesus reveal something of God's character which was

---

[11] The Greek term for this is *Christos*, from which we get the name of Jesus Christ.

hidden from the Jews in Old Testament times. It is even possible to meet some Jews who are willing to admit that Jesus' message was something new and important for deepening Israel's under- standing of God. But that is not really what Jesus taught. As far as he was concerned, he was not adding anything to the revelation of God which had already been given to Israel, and he even claimed that Abraham had seen everything which he represented about God and his purposes (John 8:52–58). Jesus said that he had come, not to reveal a new side to God's character which had not previously been understood, but to fulfil the promises already made, and thereby reinforce the truth of what people already knew (or were able to know) about him.

The newness about Jesus' revelation is not to be found at that level, but in something else altogether. What Jesus told us, and what had not previously been known, was that the one God whom we worship is a trinity of persons, each of whom can be known and worshipped within the context of a single divine being. This trinity is already implied by the narratives of Jesus' birth. He was to be called the 'Son of the Most High' (Luke 1:32) and it is stated that he was conceived by the Holy Spirit (Matt. 1:20). During his ministry on earth, Jesus scandalized the Jewish leaders of his time by calling God his Father, thereby making himself equal with God (John 5:18). He also claimed to have the power to forgive sins, a power which belongs only to God (Mark 2:5–12). Then, towards the end of his life, he told his disciples that after his departure he would send them 'another comforter', whom he immediately identified as the Holy Spirit (John 14:16–17).

It is because of these claims, and the way in which they were subsequently worked out, both in the death and resurrection of Jesus himself and in the life of the Christian church which flowed from those events, that the Christian understanding of God is quite different from that of Jews, even if in principle it is the same God whom we both worship. At the risk of oversimplifying the matter, we can say that Jews know God 'on the outside' whereas Christians know him 'on the inside'. In the Old Testament God was present among his people, but he could not be approached directly. Before Israel had a temple, God's presence was associated primarily with a large box which we call 'the ark of the covenant',[12] and anyone who touched that box was struck dead. Later on, the ark was placed in the centre of the temple, in a room known as 'the holy of holies'. No one was permitted to go into that room except the high priest, who entered it once a year bearing the sacrifice of atonement for the sins of the people. The significance of this can be seen from the fact that even now, nearly two thousand years after the last temple was destroyed, the day of atonement (Yom Kippur) is the most solemn religious holiday in the Jewish calendar.

The relative positions of Jews and non-Jews (Gentiles) were indicated in the temple by the various courts of which it was composed. There was a court for the priests, one for men, one for women and one for Gentiles. Each of these was cut off from the others and (of course) from the holy of holies. But the New Testament tells us that when Jesus died to make atonement for the sins of the whole world, these barriers came crashing down. The veil in the temple which divided the holy of holies from the rest was torn in two (Matt. 27:51). No more would the traditional distinctions between male and female, or between Jew and Gentile, be recognized, because all those who belong to Christ are regarded as Abraham's children, and therefore also as his heirs according to the promise (Gal. 3:28–29).

The Apostle Paul describes the Christian position in terms of 'access'. Whereas once we were afar off, now we have been brought near, and have been given access to the Father by Christ, in the power of the Holy Spirit (Eph. 2:18). We are 'seated in the heavenly realms in Christ Jesus' (Eph. 2:6). It is not God who has changed, but our relationship with him, which has now been placed on an entirely new footing. The basic covenant promises which were originally made to Abraham remain valid, but much of the way in which they were symbolized is now redundant. We no longer need annual sacrifices for atonement, because Christ has made a sacrifice which is valid for all time. Therefore we no

---

[12] The word 'ark' comes from the Latin *arca*, which means a large (wooden) container. It is the same word which is used to describe Noah's ark.

longer need a temple or a priesthood either. On a different level, prophets are not necessary any more, because Christ has fulfilled the prophetic word given in the Old Testament and there is no further revelation to come. Nor do we require a particular territory to live in, with all the apparatus of law and government which that would require, because Christ's kingdom is a spiritual reality which is equally present everywhere at all times.

Because of this, a good deal of the Old Testament is no longer directly applicable to us. It was designed for other circumstances, which no longer exist. But this does not mean that God has changed. He remains the Holy One of Israel, and the call to holiness is just as fundamental for Christians as it ever was for the Jews. But here again, we see what a difference the transition from 'outside' to 'inside' has made. Jews were expected to demonstrate their holiness by living separate lives. The law of Moses prescribed ritual washings and special diets which were designed to reinforce this sense of apartness – the Jews practised apartheid (and were resented for it) long before the concept was reinvented in modern times. Within the parameters of the Old Testament this not only made sense, but was insisted upon and strictly enforced by God himself. Israel's failures to achieve this goal were invariably censured, and the punishments which the nation endured were regarded as the direct result of disobedience to God's commands.

When we turn to the Christian church, we discover that although the parameters have changed, the underlying spiritual principle remains the same. Jesus taught that it was not what we eat which defiles us, but what comes out of our hearts and minds. Jewish food laws and the like were basically a waste of time from the Christian point of view, but the need to be holy was not. Jews might find it hard to understand how someone who ate meat which had been sacrificed to idols could possibly claim to be 'holy', because this obviously went against everything they had been taught, but the Apostle Paul insisted that the real issue was whether or not a person's life had been changed. True holiness did not consist in outward acts of piety but in an inward spiritual transformation, the fruits of which would be love, joy, peace, patience and so on (Gal. 5:22).

Then, as now, there were some people who went to the opposite extreme and assumed that if the outward show did not matter, and the inward disposition was essentially invisible, it was quite all right to do anything at all and still claim to be 'holy'. The Apostle Paul had to struggle against this idea on more than one occasion, which shows that it must have been widespread in the first Christian communities. Spiritual transformation, he was forced to point out, does not give us a licence to sin. On the contrary, it must lead to a changed lifestyle in which sins like fornication, stealing and so on have no place. As Jesus put it, the Christian perspective is actually much stricter in this respect than the law of Moses had been. No longer is it enough to avoid killing somebody – if we have hatred in our hearts towards another person we have 'killed' that person already and are guilty of breaking the commandment (Matt. 5:21–22). Even when it is a question of outdated customs, like observing Jewish food laws, Christians are warned not to flaunt their liberty but to respect the conscience of others and defer to their weakness if necessary (Rom. 14:13–15:1). Here as elsewhere it is not the physical act but the spiritual motive behind it which is the deciding factor.

Doing and being

There is one more factor which we have to consider before we move on from the data of revelation to the theoretical framework created out of it to form what we know as systematic theology: it is a fundamental principle of Holy Scripture that *what a person can do depends on who that person is*. This is true of Christians, for a start. If we are born again in Christ, if we have been cleansed by the blood of the Lamb, then whatever we do will reflect that holy power. 'To the pure all things are pure' (Titus 1:5). But the same verse goes on to add: 'But to those who are corrupted and who do not believe, *nothing* is pure.' The Apostle Paul says exactly the same thing to the Corinthians when he talks about eating meat which has been sacrificed to idols. Those who do this with a clear conscience have nothing to worry about, but if our consciences condemn us, then what we are doing is wrong, even if, objectively speaking, there is no harm in it (1 Cor. 8:7–13).

The same principle can be seen at work in a slightly different way in the life of Jesus. When he healed people, for example, the Pharisees did not ask him where he got the power to be able to do such miracles. They knew that he had something super-natural, but they were not interested in the mechanics of it, or in trying to acquire it for themselves. Instead, what they wanted to know is who he thought he was – 'by what authority do you do these things?' (Matt. 21:23). The Greek word for 'authority' is *exousia*, which is interesting because it is formed from the word *ousia*, which means 'being'. Literally, *exousia* is what stems from (*ex*) being. Jesus, as we know, had great fun with the Pharisees over this. He challenged them by saying that his power could come from only one of two sources – the devil or God. But if it came from the devil, how could it have such beneficial effects? If, on the other hand, it came from God, why were the God-fearing Pharisees so hostile to it? The Pharisees were confounded by this, because if they said that Jesus got his power from the devil, they would alienate the people, who knew that that could not be true. But if they admitted that it came from God, then they would be forced to follow him, and they certainly did not want to do that. So they were reduced to a politic agnosticism, which in reality was unbelief – not only in Jesus, but in God.

The same principle applies in the Old Testament, to the prom-ises which God made to Abraham and to his descendants. How could they know that God would be able to keep these promises? They could know that because of who God is. When the going got tough, that was the reality which they were called to rely on, as Isaiah 43:1–3 so vividly reminds us:

This is what the Lord says (he who created you, O Jacob, he who formed you, O Israel). 'Fear not, for I have redeemed you; I have called you by name; you are mine. When you pass through the waters, I will be with you; and when you pass through the rivers, they will not sweep over you. When you walk through the fire, you will not be burned;

the flames will not set you ablaze. For I am the Lord your God, the Holy One of Israel, your Saviour . . .'

Who God is determines what he does, and what he can do. It is for this reason that we are called to understand his being sufficiently to put our trust in his power. When we have done that, God will never abandon us, but will work in our lives and do all the things which are necessary for us to be witnesses to his glory, bringing him the honour and praise which is his due.

Summary and conclusion

This brief overview has highlighted the main points about God's self-revelation which strike us as we read the Bible. We can summarize them as follows:

1. God is the creator of everything which exists.
2. God is fully in control of his creation.
3. God has made creatures with the power to rebel against him, which some of them have done.
4. God tolerates this rebellion for a time for reasons which are not explained, but whatever the rebels may imagine, their actions cannot thwart his purposes.
5. God has revealed himself to Abraham and his descendants in a special way. Those who share Abraham's faith will be saved from the judgment to come and will enjoy God's special protection during their time on earth.
6. God's gift to Abraham cannot be revoked by human ingratitude, but neither can it be presumed upon. Israel did not choose to be saved, but neither can it rebel with impunity.
7. In Jesus Christ, God fulfilled the promises made to Abraham and the other leading figures of the Old Testament. In the process he revealed himself as a trinity of persons with whom his people can now enter into relationship.
8. Because of what Christ has done, Christians are privileged to enter into the inner life of God in a way which was not possible

for Jews. This transforms our relationship with him, not because he changes in any way but because we move much closer to the heart of his being. This in turn means that the demands placed on us to be like God in his holiness have a new and deeper application in our lives, without changing the fundamental principle which established them in the first place.

Bearing these points in mind, we can now turn our attention to the philosophical issues which revelation raises.

3

'I Am What I Am' – The Ontological Imperative

Is revelation necessary?

The Bible claims to be a revelation of God, but do we need such a thing? Can we not discover all that we need to know about God from examining the world around us? There are plenty of people who think that we can, and they sit light to the demands of the church. These are the types who believe that they can worship God on the golf course just as easily as in the pew, who claim that their religion is 'the Sermon on the Mount' (which they have probably never read) and who think that if they do their best it will all work out in the end, whatever happens. What can we say about that?

The Bible seems to give us some encouragement to believe that God can be seen in nature. Psalm 19, for example, says:

> The heavens declare the glory of God; the skies proclaim the work of his hands.
> Day after day they pour forth speech; night after night they display knowledge.
> There is no speech or language where their voice is not heard.
> Their voice goes out into all the earth, their words to the ends of the world.

(1–4)

It would appear from this that anyone who looks at the world around us can come to the conclusion that there must be a Supreme

Being behind it all. We are even told that every person has a conscience which tells him the difference between right and wrong, and that this conscience is the equivalent of God's law (Rom. 2:14–15). Going further still, the Apostle Paul is prepared to remark that nobody has any excuse, because from the beginning of the world everyone has known God to some degree (Rom. 1:20–21). All this is true, but what it tells us is that we can know by nature that there is a God, and that he functions according to certain principles which we call 'morality'. This is fine as far as it goes, but it is not enough to bring us to the saving knowledge which we have received in Christ. For us to know God in that way, he has to encounter us personally, and tell us himself what he is like.

Personal knowledge is always like this. Let me illustrate with a simple example. I know that there is a man who stands next to me at the bus stop every morning, and I can say quite a lot about him from what I have observed. But I do not know him personally, and never shall, unless I communicate with him – and more importantly, unless he communicates with me. I might then discover that a lot of what I 'knew' about him before was really no more than the product of my imagination. For example, because he does not wear a wedding ring, I assume that he is single, but in fact he may be happily married. Because he is black, I assume that he comes from Africa, but he could easily be West Indian or even American. And so on. This is what knowledge of God without revelation is like – we can see something, and what we see is 'true' in its way, but we have no way of knowing whether we have interpreted it correctly or not. Only revelation can help us with that. The limits of natural theology can perhaps best be expressed in the words of a popular chorus:

Jesus is Lord, creation's voice proclaims it
For by his power each tree and flower was planned and made.
Jesus is Lord, the universe declares it
Sun, moon and stars in heaven cry 'Jesus is Lord'.

The author of this ditty has combined Psalm 19 with Philippians 2:11, and his intentions were no doubt of the best. But what he has ended up with is not only unbiblical, it is heretical. For the sun, moon and stars do *not* cry 'Jesus is Lord' – you cannot come to a knowledge of redemption simply by looking at the works of creation. So in the end we have to disagree with the pious Sunday golfer – what he can see is something, to be sure, but it is not enough to get him to heaven.

At this point it might be worth saying something about the so-called 'proofs for the existence of God'. These are arguments which have been devised by philosophers as ways of demonstrating that there must be a God who corresponds to the God of the Bible. One of them argues that because the world consists of different kinds of beings, there must be a supreme being that is greater than any of the others. This being is God. Another says that just as a watch needs a watchmaker, so the universe needs a creator, who is also God. And so on. All of them have been refuted at one time or another, and a recent defence of them does no more than argue that collectively they provide a strong argument in favour of the existence of God, without actually proving it.[13]

The snag with these 'proofs' is that they have been devised by people who already believe in the Christian God and whose main aim is to justify that belief. This does not make the effort worthless, of course, but it changes its nature. It cannot be said that the proofs are persuasive to those who do not believe, and few people (if any) have been converted by them. Their most useful function is to fortify the faith of those who believe already on other grounds, and those grounds must be those provided by revelation. Philosophical constructs are useful in their place, but as the medieval theologians used to say, philosophy is the handmaid of theology, not its mistress, and certainly not a substitute for it.

From revelation to theology

Is there any need to go beyond what the Bible says about God? In one sense, of course, the answer to this question must be 'no'.

---

[13] R. Swinburne, *The Existence of God* (Oxford, 1981).

Everything that we know about God is revealed in Scripture, and even if this knowledge can be confirmed by other things, such as observing the natural universe or listening to the testimony of people who have encountered him in their lives, we shall not learn anything that we could not already have said on the basis of the Bible. Indeed, we must use the Bible to determine whether (or to what extent) these other evidences are reliable.

That much is clear. But the Bible does not come to us in a systematic format, laid out in a logical order with a ready answer to every question. This might not matter if all we had to do was to read it and appreciate it as a literary text, but if we are expected to use it as a practical guide to life, it is very helpful to have some kind of index or concordance which will tell us where to find certain things. Such an index is bound to be systematic in presentation, since it would otherwise be impossible to use. And once we start creating a systematic index, we have headed down the road towards systematic theology.

What does this do to our understanding of the God of the Bible, who has not revealed himself to us in that way? Basically there are three possible options, which can be set out as follows.

A. *A change of form means that there is automatically a change of substance as well.* This argument is popular nowadays, and is held by people who subscribe to the view that 'the medium is the message'. It may well be the basic conviction of at least some of the authors of *The Openness of God*, even though it is a dangerously absolute position to hold. Everyday experience would suggest that it is perfectly possible to change the form of some things (putty springs to mind) without altering the substance, and caution would suggest that it is best to keep this option open.

B. *A change of form does not necessarily entail a change of substance, but in the case of theology that is what has in fact happened.* This is certainly the position held by the authors of *The Openness of God*, whether it is undergirded by A or not. The result, according to them, is a distortion of our perception which has done great harm to our understanding of God, and therefore also to our relationship with him.

C. *A change of form does not necessarily entail a change of substance, and in the case of theology this has not happened.* This is the traditional position, which has been argued one way or another since ancient times. According to those who hold this view, systematic theology is useful as a guide to revelation. Its main function is to prevent us from interpreting one part of God's Word in a way which is inconsistent with other parts. It also helps us to see things we might otherwise overlook, because it is not possible to keep the entire Bible in mind all the time. If there is a discrepancy between the data of revelation and the index known as systematic theology, then it is the index which must be changed. This happens from time to time, but it must be said that it does not occur easily or often. The index can always be improved, but its basic style and content have stood the test of time and been found reliable by very different users. Those who want to discard it altogether have therefore got to make a very good case for their point of view.

Systematic theology has got itself a bad name in some circles because those who practise it are suspected of having created a theoretical framework which does not correspond to the facts. Sometimes theologians may try to answer questions which the Bible does not discuss, such as, what was God doing before he made the world?[14] They may over-systematize, and end up by saying things which are purely speculative and have no real basis in revelation. On the other hand, theologians may also be too selective in their treatment of Scripture, taking passages which suit what they want to say and ignoring others. This is one of the things which the authors of *The Openness of God* accuse the classical theological tradition of having done. According to them, traditional theology has concentrated on a string of Bible verses which appear to substantiate the belief that God is immutable, impassible, incomprehensible and so on, to the exclusion of other verses which remind us that he cares about his people, that he listens to our prayers, and that he adapts himself to changing

---

[14] Augustine (350–430) answered this one by saying that God was busily making hell for people who asked such questions!

circumstances. As a result, they claim, God has been reduced to something less than he truly is, and if we follow this teaching we shall be cut off from a vital part of our relationship with him.

In response to this, the first thing that must be said is that the Bible presents us with only one God, who is consistent and coherent in himself. This does not mean that he can be easily understood, as if he were just a kind of mathematical symbol or something like that. There are many aspects to God's being, and there is much about him that we shall never understand. This may sound discouraging at first, but just consider human beings. We know all kinds of other people, but how deeply do we understand them? Indeed, how deeply do we understand ourselves? If modern psychology has taught us anything, it is that we do not know ourselves very well at all. So how can we expect to have a deep understanding of God?

Of course this does not mean that we cannot 'know' him in any way at all. People who meet me know that I am a white European male with brown hair and blue eyes, and they recognize me when they see me. They have some idea of what I am like and within limits they know what to expect from me. But not always, and there are many sides to me of which they have no knowledge or understanding at all. The same, of course, applies to every one of us, but we would not therefore say that we are unknown or unknowable.

When other people meet us, they see us as we are – there is not some invisible part of our being lurking behind the curtains, waiting to pop out at the unsuspecting guest. But at the same time, their knowledge of us is superficial. If it is based on observation only, it may also be highly mistaken. Very often, we are dependent on what other people tell us about themselves in order to understand something more about them. But even that is not reliable, since people do not always tell the truth about themselves, and what they say is invariably slanted – usually in a way which is flattering to them. For example, I may say that I am a fast, efficient worker, but someone else might think that what this really means is that I am impatient and intolerant of others who get in the way. Have I lied about myself? No, but I have not told the full truth either, and the wise person will be cautious about relying too much on such testimony. When it comes to knowing God, however, we can rely on what he says about himself because his own self-understanding is perfect. But on the other hand, we have no guarantee that we have been told the full story, and Scripture in fact tells us that we have not. There are hidden depths in God's being which have not been revealed to us and which we shall never see, but that does not invalidate what we have been told, nor does it mean that we have never really had an encounter with the living God.

What is important for systematic theology is that we should have an understanding of God which is consistent and coherent, even if it cannot be exhaustive. For example, we cannot have a picture of God which says that sometimes he is in control of the universe but sometimes he is not. Unfortunately, this is precisely what many people think. If something good happens to them, they may regard it as 'an answer to prayer', which implies that God has intervened on their behalf and used his sovereign power in a way which only he can do. But if something bad happens to them, they may think that the devil or some other force opposed to his will has taken over and done something which God himself either let happen or was powerless to prevent.

Curiously enough, this attitude is at its most powerful when we are speaking about conversion. Many people pray for the conversion of others, assuming that God can bring this about. But these same people also believe that every human being is free to accept or reject God as he or she sees fit. They do not seem to realize that it is illogical to pray for something if at the same time they assume that it is not in God's power to deliver it! But this behaviour is very common, and many people get upset when someone points out that it does not make sense. If the truth be told, very often this is the real reason why they do not like systematic theology – it challenges their own inconsistencies and disturbs what they want to believe, whether it is true or not.

Theology is not the only discipline to suffer from this phenomenon. Medicine is another area where 'old wives' tales' are extraordinarily popular and difficult to dislodge, and perhaps the similarity with theology is not coincidental. It may be that when our own well-being is at stake we are somehow more inclined to trust our own intuitions, or even rely on our own fantasies, than we are to accept the advice of a so-called 'expert', particularly if that advice is not what we want to hear. There is always one chain-smoker who lives to be 100, and many people would rather quote that exception than pay attention to the depressing statistics to which they are much more likely to belong!

A true systematic theology, one which is faithful to its data, will not go beyond Scripture but will seek to provide a framework within which Scripture can be understood. It is not constructed in a haphazard fashion, but according to a method which proceeds from the clearer statements of the Bible to the more obscure ones, and seeks to understand the latter in the light of the former.

As an example of this, we may look again at the creation. It is quite clear in the Bible that God made the world and that one day he will bring it to an end. But there are evil forces in the world which are opposed to his will. Did God create them as well? The logic of creation says that he must have done so, since otherwise they would not exist, or else they would be God's equals and God would not be the ultimate reality. Did he then create them evil? Again, the logic of creation says no – whatever God creates is good. So how do these forces end up being evil? The answer must be that God created them with the freedom to disobey his will. Does that mean that God planned their disobedience? Here we are inclined to say no, but if he did not do so, how could they have rebelled in a world controlled by the power of God? Hard as it is to accept, it is easier to believe that God somehow planned this rebellion than it is to believe that his creatures did something against his will, but which he was for some reason powerless to prevent.

Can these rebellious creatures be blamed for something which was planned by God? Here the answer must be yes, because a creature which is not responsible for its actions is not truly free. There is no point denying that this is a great mystery, which offends our human sense of fairness and justice. The only way I can begin to understand it is to look at myself. I want to be free, and resent it when I am forced to do what others want against my own will, even if there are good objective reasons for believing that obedience will be to my benefit. Sometimes I go against the wishes of others for no better reason than that I am determined to demonstrate my independence. Logic, reason and common sense have nothing to do with this; it is 'freedom' which matters to me, even if I know that I shall have to pay a price for it. Why do I behave like this? I have no idea, but experience has shown me that it is a fact. And experience has shown us all that this is a common human trait. Trying to make sense of it is beside the point, because often it makes no sense at all. But denying it is even more foolish, because it is a fact of life with which we have to cope every day.

The conclusion of all this is that God is in sovereign control of the universe – nothing escapes his power. But he is not responsible for evil, even though he has created beings who rebel against him and in some sense has planned that rebellion. It is an unfathomable mystery as to why this should be so, but alternative explanations are worse because they fail to do justice to the power of God. Does God realize that we have a problem with this? Of course he does, and he gives us an answer as well. Look at Romans 9:18–23:

> God has mercy on whom he wants to have mercy, and he hardens whom he wants to harden. One of you will say to me: 'Then why does God still blame us? For who resists his will?' But who are you, O man, to talk back to God? Shall what is formed say to him who formed it, 'Why did you make me like this?' Does not the potter have the right to make out of the same lump of clay some pottery for noble purposes and some for common use? What if God, choosing to show his wrath and make his power known, bore with great patience the objects of his wrath – prepared for destruction? What if he did this to make the riches of his glory known to the objects of his mercy, whom he prepared in advance for glory?

There is no inconsistency or injustice in God, because ultimately he is the sovereign creator, who can do whatever he likes. He is who he is – and that takes us right to the heart of what the Bible tells us about him.

The name and identity of God

When we turn from the basic data of the biblical revelation to the implications which it has for our beliefs, we have to begin with the name of God as this is revealed in Exodus 3. According to the most usual translation of the Hebrew, God declares to Moses that his name is I AM, and this is confirmed by the way in which it is translated in the Greek of the New Testament. It is sometimes claimed that the name 'Yahweh', which is the usual pronunciation given to the Hebrew letters (all consonants) does not in fact derive from the verb 'to be', but even if that is true it is hardly relevant to the theological discussion. Wherever the name originally came from, it was understood to mean 'he who is', and that must be regarded as its significance for biblical religion.

Similarly, the argument that what God said to Moses was 'I shall be what I shall be' and not 'I am what I am', which is also sometimes put forward, does not stand up to serious investigation. It rests on the fact that the Hebrew verb does not have a tense system, but relies instead on what are called 'aspects'. There are two of these – an aspect denoting completed action (technically known as the 'perfective') and an aspect denoting uncompleted action (technically known as the 'imperfective'). Normally it might be supposed that present and future actions, being uncompleted by definition, would be in the imperfective aspect, but this is not necessarily the case. It all depends on the standpoint of the speaker, or on the main clause in the sentence. If, for example, I say in English: 'If I *came* tomorrow, would you be at home?' I am supposing that the action of my coming will precede my discovery of your being at home, and therefore I can express it as 'completed', even if it is in the future!

In the Hebrew sentence 'I am what I am' the imperfective aspect is necessary because the action being described has not been finished. There is no suggestion that it has not yet begun, nor that it implies that there will be some kind of change in the future. If a meaning of that kind were intended, Hebrew would have to indicate as much by adding either some other word (like 'soon') which would make the sentence future in meaning, or another clause which put it in that time framework. As neither of these things is the case, we must assume that the present tense is the right way to translate this into English. Interestingly enough, the Greek translators of the Old Testament, working about two centuries before the birth of Christ, preferred to render the meaning by using the Greek present participle (*hōn*, literally 'the being') which they evidently felt was better than the present tense of the verb, and this form is taken up in the New Testament book of Revelation (1:8).[15] For practical purposes therefore, we may conclude that the traditional translation is the right one and work from it. What does it imply? First of all, it means that God has a reality in himself which is permanent, and which is unqualified by any other factor. He does not depend on anything else for his existence, nor does he have to do anything to prove it – he is simply there, as a given fact. Furthermore, there is no sign that there is any beginning or end to his being.

This is an important point, because it brings us to the question of time and eternity. Within the world of time, everything has a beginning, and we may suppose that it will have an end as well, even if that is less clear. But God does not dwell within the world of time, even if he is active in it. This is a point which many people find hard to grasp, and so we must look at it carefully. Time is measured by three tenses – past, present and future. We think we know what these are, although in fact they are changing all the time. To put it crudely, the past is getting longer and the future is getting shorter, at least in the sense that the future is constantly becoming the past. But what about the present? How do we define that? For most people, the 'present' includes whatever is continuous from the recent past and can be assumed to apply into the foreseeable future. This may have little relation to actual time. For example, if I say that at present Queen Elizabeth II is on the throne, what I mean is that the last time I heard, she was still reigning, and I expect her to continue to do so for the time being, unless something drastic occurs. The fact that she has been on the

---

[15] This is then retranslated into English using the present tense ('he who is') because it is not natural for us to use the participle ('he is being') in this way!

throne since 1952 does not matter – she is still there now (as far as I know). On the other hand, the Soviet Union, which was alive and well in 1952, is now part of the past because it has ceased to exist. It is not something that I am going to have to deal with tomorrow, even if I wish to, whereas it is at least possible that I might meet the queen. The fact that the two were contemporary for nearly forty years is completely irrelevant.

In human terms therefore, what is 'present' is basically what each of us has to take into account as a living reality, which may confront us at some point in the future. But strictly speaking, there is no 'present' in time at all. If I try to define the 'present' moment, it is past as soon as I open my mouth. In reality therefore, the 'present' has only notional existence. It is an idea which helps me to focus on what still matters from the past as I look ahead to what is coming. Does this mean that it does not matter?

Certainly not! Far from being inconsequential, the 'present' is fundamental to the way I live. This becomes most obvious when we meet people who are 'living in the past'. They are not in a different historical time to the one we live in, but past events which have ceased to have any meaning for us are still functionally present in their lives. We notice this (and usually disapprove of it) only because the things which are real to them no longer have any practical significance for us, and (we assume) ought not to have any practical significance for them either. A very common example of this is the tendency some people have to deny the death of a loved one. A parent or a spouse goes on 'living' in the minds of some people, even when everybody else knows that they are dead. This is perceived as a sad, and even tragic, situation because such a belief is unlikely to have a positive effect on the actions which these people will take in the future. We fear that with their perspective they are likely to make the wrong choices, influenced by something which has ceased to be real in objective fact but which continues to possess their minds.

It is in the light of this that we have to consider the significance of God's 'presence'. Obviously it means that he is a being with whom we must reckon as we look towards the future, since we shall have to deal with him at every stage along our journey in life. But how far does this also involve an appropriation of the past? Does what has already happened have a bearing on our calculations, and if so, to what extent? Here the Christian claim is truly breathtaking. Christians say that *everything* which has happened or will happen matters, because it is all 'present' in God. This may be hard to picture, but perhaps the human memory provides some kind of analogy. People who 'live in the past' can often recount significant events in their lives in great detail. They will remember, for example, that it was because the mechanic did a poor job that the brakes failed, that the accident happened, that somebody was killed, and so on. The process of cause and effect is not suppressed – it is very important – but each stage is 'present' just as much as the others are. Nor is it necessarily true that the person's actions now are determined only by the final result, because any or every stage in the process may send its particular message to them. We avoid the garage with the bad mechanic, we check the brakes daily, and so on.

The memory's ability to give equal weight to a whole series of individual events, and at the same time to respect the process of cause and effect (and therefore of time) which connects them, may be a picture which gives us some idea of how God's mind might work. At least it allows us to imagine the possibility of concentrating on particular things without losing sight of the process – in the memory, time is abstracted but its significance does not disappear. If the future seems to be more problematic than the past because it is not in our memory, that is only true from our perspective. God stands at the end of time, just as he is the creator of its beginning. In him there is no past or future, because everything is eternally 'present' in his mind. At the end of the day, as at the beginning, he is the Alpha and the Omega, the beginning and the end, the great I AM (Rev. 1:8).

What is God like?

If we accept the objective existence of an eternal God, what can we say about him? In particular, can we really say that he is immutable if he is a living being, who maintains an equally living relationship with his all-too-mutable creatures? Before we get too far into this, we have to take a quick look at terminology, because it is easy to get confused at this point. So far we have been talking about God's *being* or 'essence'. Now we are moving on to talk about his *nature*, or what his essence is like. Traditionally, theologians have concluded that, for all practical purposes, God's being and his nature are one and the same thing. They have argued that because God is perfect, his 'goodness' (for example) must be equally perfect and therefore coterminous with his being. It is therefore possible to call God 'the Good One' because goodness is a quality which extends to the fulness of his being.

All this may be true, but it is still important for us to maintain a distinction between being and nature. In human terms, this is quite clear, because the two things are not coterminous. Nobody would suggest, for example, that 'human being' and 'human nature' are synonyms! We understand that what we are like is different from what we are, even if the two things are closely related and inseparable in practice. In the case of God, his being and his nature are so close to one another that when we talk about the latter we automatically encompass the former as well, but even so a distinction between them must be maintained. This is because God's being is unfathomable and hidden from our eyes, whereas his nature is at least partially revealed to us. What we say about his nature helps us to understand his being, but it cannot fully explain it. For example, we can call God fully and absolutely the ultimate Good, but he still has a number of other characteristics which are not included in this designation, but which are equally important in their own way. We must not assume that by calling God good we have said all there is to say about the divine being.

The importance of this distinction becomes even clearer when we look at how we normally describe God's nature. We say, for example, that he is invisible, immortal, infinite and so on. But what do these words actually mean? Very little in fact. To be 'invisible' simply means that something cannot be seen. God is invisible, but then so are leprechauns and atoms. Are we to conclude from this that God is fictitious or that he is too small to be seen with the naked eye? Clearly not, but the word 'invisible' is sufficiently elastic in its meaning to allow for both of those possibilities. All we are really saying is that God cannot be limited or defined in such a way as to make him accessible to human vision. He is not a creature and therefore cannot be confined within the framework of time and space. But what he is in positive terms remains unknown.

Of course it will be obvious to those who pause to think about it that what we are doing here is defining the word 'invisible' in such a way that it will suit what we already believe about God. This is exactly what we do with every word which we use to describe his nature. When we say that God is 'immutable' we mean no more than that *in himself* he is the same, yesterday, today and for ever. He remains sovereign, almighty, eternal, holy and so on. We are not saying anything about the way in which he relates to us, which may well vary considerably according to circumstances. A parent who cuddles a child one minute and spanks him the next is still the same parent, and the relationship between the two remains unchanged. Indeed, it is precisely because the relationship is constant that the actual behaviour varies in the way that it does, because it is the parent's duty to nurture and discipline the child. There is no contradiction here, and no 'change', except in outward appearance. So it is in our relationship with God. 'Change', such as it is, is superficial, and more apparent than real. The underlying principles which govern the relationship remain the same.

It is very similar when we come to talk about God's 'moral' qualities. To look at what we have just said, what does it mean to say that God is 'good'? Every Christian will agree that this is a true statement, but it is only meaningful for God to be 'good' in contrast to something else which is not good. If God is considered simply by himself, the word 'good' is meaningless, because there is nothing to compare it with.

This may seem like a trivial point to some people, but actually it is very important. Everything which God does must reflect the goodness of his nature, since otherwise it would not be a divine act. But what if God decides to send a famine, or a plague? Is that good? Here we are faced squarely with the relativity of the concept. 'Good' in relation to what? Let us take a very common example. In the Book of Common Prayer there is a prayer for rain, followed immediately by another prayer for fair weather. In the largely agricultural society of sixteenth-century England, we can imagine that most people would have been praying for the same thing at the same time, because what was good and necessary to them depended entirely on the crops. Today, on the other hand, there is major conflict of interest between farmers and city-dwellers on this point. Farmers want rain when townies want sunshine, because the former are planting crops while the latter are either heading to the seaside or organizing garden parties. Which of these things is 'good'? In this situation, God cannot please everybody at the same time, but does this mean that he is imperfect, untrustworthy or bad? Of course not. All it means is that we have defined 'good' according to criteria which are inadequate to do justice to him, and if we judge him by those we are bound to come up with a false impression of what he is really like.

From all of this we must conclude that even true statements about God are false or meaningless if they are taken out of context, and that context is his unknowable being. In other words, he defines the parameters by which we are to understand the meaning of the words which we use to describe him. Anything else will give the wrong picture and produce more confusion than enlightenment. Nothing illustrates this point more clearly than the classic statement that 'God is love'. The authors of *The Openness of God* maintain that this is the key to understanding who and what God is, and it is to this that we must now turn our attention.

God is love

What does it mean to say that 'God is love'? Like the statement that 'God is good' it is meaningless by itself, because God can only be love in relation to something else. Love is not an objectively existing thing, but a quality which is discerned in relationships. For the love of God to have any meaning, there must be something (or someone) for him to love, and the meaning of the word will be determined by the nature of the relationship thus established.

In the Bible, God is described as loving primarily in relation to his covenant people. It is a special quality which is visible in that context, and which stands in sharp contrast to the relationship which God has with others, a relationship which may even be described as hatred. We are not meant to conclude from this that God has an aversion to everything which is outside his covenant, or that he is at best indifferent to the fate of those whom he has not chosen. God does not hate anything that he has made, as his tolerant preservation of the world in the face of its sin and rebellion indicates. But neither is it right to say that he 'loves' it in the same way that he loves his chosen people. Here we come face to face with two different kinds of relationship, and therefore also with two different kinds of love. This need not cause a problem, as long as we remember that it is the former which determines the latter.

This may seem odd at first sight, but it becomes clear when we think of how human love shows the same variations. Consider the following: I love my parents, I love my wife, I love my children, I love my brothers and sisters, I love my friends. Are we talking about the same thing when we use the word 'love' in this way? Of course not. I have sexual intercourse with my wife, which is perfectly appropriate in the context of loving her. But if I were to have sex with my mother, my daughter or my sister it would be an abomination – worse even, than having sex with a friend. Does this mean that I love my wife more than my mother or my daughter? No. The relationship is different, and so the love between us is correspondingly different too. Once again, it is the nature of the relationship which determines what 'love' will mean in any particular context.

This can have very serious consequences if categories get confused, as they sometimes do. What are we to make of it when a man says that his wife is his best friend, for example? Are we to conclude from this that he has sexual relations with all his friends? This may seem absurd, but it is precisely because these things have been confused in modern life that many people today assume that any deep relationship must involve sexual contact, so much so that in some contexts the word 'love' has come to be virtually synonymous with 'sex'. This is a very serious perversion of the word 'love', not because the two things are *never* connected, but because it is an unacceptably narrow definition of the word, which either excludes the greater part of human experience or else turns it into immorality.

We have to bear all this in mind very carefully when we come to define what we mean when we say that 'God is love'. Such a concept is only meaningful in the context of an established relationship, and not all of God's relationships are alike. Having said that, we may go on to add that his relationships with believers are fundamentally the same, because the salvation to which we have been called is one reality in Christ. Even so, however, what is basically a single thing is manifested in many different ways, because our individual situations vary so much from one another. God may reward me for faithfulness in one thing but at the same time punish me for disobedience in another. He may apply the same principle to someone else but in a way which looks completely different to an outside observer, because that someone has different needs and different problems to overcome.

Anyone who has ever engaged in pastoral ministry knows this. One of the hardest things to learn when listening to other people's troubles is to remember that they belong to someone else, not to us. At one extreme, this means that we must not sympathize with such people to the point where we fantasize ourselves into their position, even as we try to understand where they are coming from. We cannot legitimately 'identify' with others to that extent, nor would it be right if we could. People who are in serious need do not want to be understood – they want to be helped, and it is not usually possible to do this if we (who presumably want to help) try to take the problem on ourselves. Think of a doctor approaching a sick patient. Does the patient want the doctor to contract his disease, out of 'solidarity' with him, or does he want the doctor to cure it? The answer is surely obvious. At the other end of the scale, there are many problems which seem trivial to us because they are not ours. I listen to my students complain about how hard they find it to master a subject with which I am quite familiar. What is wrong with them?, I sometimes think. But I would be failing in my duty as a teacher if I did not accept that they have certain difficulties which have to be addressed, however 'simple' they may seem to me. And of course, the last thing a student wants to hear is that his teacher does not know the answer either!

Love in these cases has to include confrontation and correction, which will take different forms according to the need, but whose final end is the same – to produce healthy and educated people. When we look at God's love we find something similar. Because of our needs, he is often a doctor and a teacher to us, confronting our rebelliousness and correcting our sins, so that we may become what he wants us to be – holy people reflecting his glory in the world. But in discussing this we often come up against the same kind of category confusion which we mentioned earlier. Very often, people talk about God in terms which describe him as a 'friend'. This is not an unbiblical way of speaking, but it can be very misleading because of the way we normally understand friendship.

Friends are people whom we regard as equals and with whom we share common interests and pursuits. We bond with them precisely because of our similarities, and if these turn out to be less (or less important) than we first imagined, the friendship will suffer as a result and may even be terminated. But God is not a friend in this sense, nor can he be. We are not his equals, and we do not bond with him because of common interests which we happen to share. On the contrary, the Bible says that it was while we were still sinners that Christ died for us (Rom. 5:8). This is hardly what one would call mutual attraction! And Jesus says quite explicitly that he calls us his friends *if we do whatever he commands us* (John 15:14). This is very different from the normal kind of human friendship, and much more like a parent–child or teacher–pupil relationship. Once again, we find that the terms we use are defined by the nature of the relationship, not the other way round. Unfortunately, many people fail to see this, and so they develop not only a wrong picture but (worse) unrealistic expectations of God. It is not surprising if this all leads to grave disappointment, but the answer to that is surely not to abandon the traditional view of God. The fault does not lie with the doctrine but with our perception, which has been skewed by false, inappropriate or inadequate definitions of terms. It is to that issue that we must now turn our attention.

Talking about God

So far we have been talking about God principally from a biblical standpoint. But as we have looked into this more deeply, we have found it helpful to classify the biblical data in terms like *being* and *nature*. The Bible itself does not make this kind of abstraction, but the substance of what these words are trying to express is certainly found in Scripture. It is very important to know what kind of being God is, since if we get that wrong we shall misunderstand what he is saying to us and our relationship with him will suffer as a consequence. But here we come up against the objection that the terms which we normally use to describe God are drawn from the inheritance of Greek philosophy, not from the Scriptures themselves. This leads some to assume that these terms must somehow be inappropriate. Either we are saying things about God which are not really true or we are saying true things in such a way as to distort what the Bible is trying to tell us. Whatever the case may be, the result is a picture of God which amounts to an intellectual idol and is not a faithful representation of the truth.

This charge is a serious one, but it is by no means new. The fathers of the First Council of Nicaea (AD 325) had to contend with those who objected to using the word *homoousios* ('consubstantial') of the Son in relation to the Father, because this word is not in the Bible. John Calvin lashed out in his *Institutes* (I. 13) against those who refused to accept terms like 'person' and 'trinity' for the same reason. He argued that if the realities these words are meant to describe are found in Scripture, then we can use the terms as a kind of intellectual shorthand, because we have a common understanding of what they are meant to convey. More recently, the same general objection has been made again, but this time it is backed up by a broader attack on the theological tradition generally, which we have already mentioned. The charge now is that not only words, but thought-patterns and ideas have crept in from an alien source, and polluted the pure waters of the biblical spring.

How valid is this criticism? First of all, let it be admitted that many of the words which we use in theology do in fact come from a pagan Greek philosophical source. The word 'theology' is a case in point. It was probably invented by Plato, who used it in his *Republic* to mean what we would now call 'mythology'. This is not surprising, because the gods whom he was talking about were understood in mythological terms. Plato did not believe that there was any serious connection between the Greek myths and the worship of the Supreme Being. What he seems to have thought is that mythology (or 'theology' as he put it) was a popular explanation of reality intended for the ignorant and uneducated. Those who progressed to the heights of philosophical reasoning could sort the wheat from the chaff in the myths, and distil the pure truth of Reason. This could then be applied to such things as the Homeric poems, which could be interpreted (or 'deconstructed' as we might say today) to reveal their underlying rational basis. The process by which this was done is known today as 'allegory', and it quickly became a favourite means of reading ancient Greek literature in the philosophical schools of antiquity.

'Theology' is not a word found in the Bible, possibly because it would have meant 'mythology' to most readers of the New Testament and been misunderstood accordingly. But there is no doubt that the Bible speaks about God, and so does contain a theology, as long as this term is understood in relation to the God it describes and not in the context of Greek paganism. Once again, we see that the thing being described determines the parameters of the term being used to describe it, and not the other way round. Christians eventually came to use the word 'theology' in a way which applied to the God of the Bible, which automatically gave it a radically different content from what had been customary before. The Bible does not speak of God in mythological terms, decipherable only by a process of allegory. On the contrary, it talks straightforwardly about God and the nature of his being, making Christian theology appear much closer to Greek philosophy than to Greek religion or 'theology'.

Perhaps the word was borrowed from Plato, but this does not mean that Platonists recognized its use by Christians. On the contrary, most of them ridiculed Christianity as an irrational and barbaric superstition making absurd claims, which could in no sense be dignified with philosophical or pseudo-philosophical terminology. But along with the ridicule went imitation. Little though they would admit it, the Neoplatonists of the third and fourth centuries AD absorbed more of Christianity than most people realize. As far as the word 'theology' is concerned, the climax was reached in the work of Proclus (*c.* 411–85), who wrote a book called *The Elements of Theology* in which he used the word in its Christian, not its Platonic, meaning. Proclus wanted to show that it was possible to describe Plato's belief in a supreme Reason as a form of monotheism, but this was really a covert concession to the Christian world-view, since Plato would not have used the word 'theology' in that way.

What is true of 'theology' is paradigmatic of the entire relationship between Christianity and ancient Greek philosophy. The Greeks used words like 'being' (*ousia*), 'nature' (*physis*) and 'substance' (*hypostasis*) in many different ways. In his book *Divine Substance*[16] Christopher Stead demonstrated, by citing a wide range of examples, that these terms had no fixed meaning in Greek thought. On the contrary, they were used in ways which were often vague and imprecise, causing problems for subsequent interpreters and allowing competing schools of disciples to claim that they were all following their chosen master(s). Precision in vocabulary did not come until Christians imposed it on themselves, because they had a definable God whom they needed to describe accurately. When Christians spoke of God as the 'supreme being' they were not speculating about some abstract idea;

---

[16] (Oxford, 1977).

they were trying to describe someone whom they already knew by personal experience.

The imprecision of existing Greek terminology was a hindrance to this, and the church had to sort it out in order to avoid misunderstandings. The word *ousia* had to be confined to the oneness of God's being, because to use it of the Father, Son and Holy Spirit would imply that there were three gods. The word *hypostasis*, on the other hand, came to be used of the persons of the trinity, even though there were initially many people who thought of it as basically synonymous with *ousia*. This caused problems in the Latin world, because when *ousia* was translated as *essentia* the Romans rejected it.[17] Instead, they preferred to say *substantia*. As long as nobody saw any real difference between *ousia* and *hypostasis* this was no problem, but Christian theology forced Roman believers to define their terms more precisely. Tertullian (*fl. c.* 196–212) used *substantia* for *ousia*, but then he took a completely different word, which had never been used by any philosopher, and employed it for expressing the threeness of God. This was the word *persona*, which we still use (in its English form 'person') today.

Tertullian meant by *persona* what his Greek counterparts meant by *hypostasis*, but the Greeks did not understand or accept this for a long time. To them, the word *prosōpon* (*persona* in Latin) meant 'mask' and was mainly used in the theatre. The Greeks imagined that Tertullian and his followers believed that the Father, Son and Holy Spirit were merely masks worn by God in the drama of human history, and that they did not represent genuinely distinct beings. This was the heresy known as 'modalism'[18] which they naturally rejected. It was not until Basil of Caesarea (*c.* 329–79) realized that the Latin terminology was different from the Greek, but that the underlying doctrine was the same, that the way towards a reconciliation was opened up.

---

[17] This happened in the first century BC, and had nothing to do with Christianity.

[18] Or 'Sabellianism', after a certain Sabellius, who was supposed to have preached it.

Finally, the Council of Chalcedon (AD 451) declared that *hypostasis* and *persona* were synonymous, and so they have remained ever since.

The important point here is that no pagan philosopher could have spoken in these terms. A Greek would not have said that God (or anything else) was one *ousia* in three *hypostases* because he would not have understood what the distinction between these terms was supposed to be. He might have been able to accept it once it was explained (as many in fact did), but that explanation depended on the preaching of the Christian gospel which made the distinction meaningful in the first place. A Roman would never have concluded that God was three *personae* in one *substantia*, because to his mind the terms belonged to different worlds. The first one came from the theatre and had been introduced into the law, whereas the second was primarily philosophical. It could be used in a legal context as well, but not in a way which had any relationship to the use of *persona*. It could mean a material thing, or property, as it does for example in the AV rendering of Luke 15:13, where the prodigal son is described as 'wasting his substance in riotous living'. It would hardly have made sense to say that the persons of the Godhead might do the same with their 'substance', and so once again we find that without a prior acceptance of the Christian message, the terminology used in Christian theology would not have made sense to those who were accustomed to using the same words in other ways.

Once again, we find ourselves coming back to the same principle which we have seen at work elsewhere. *The reality which is being described defines the parameters of meaning appropriate to the terminology used to describe it.* This does not mean that the words we use are totally unsuitable to begin with. For example, a word like 'salt' or 'jabberwocky' has nothing to commend it in advance as a possible description of God, and we would not think of making use of either of them. But given that we can find words which have the potential for saying something meaningful about him, the precise definition which will turn these words into technical terms is shaped to a considerable extent by the nature of the subject under discussion. This is not obscurantism, as some might think, but the normal practice of every scientific discipline. The word 'infinity' for example, means something different to a mathematician from what it means to a theologian. In mathematics 'infinity' is really a finite term implying no more than indefinite extension (e.g. 'Between the numbers 1 and 2 there is an infinity of fractions.') No theologian would use the word like this, even if there is some overlap in meaning which makes the different usages comprehensible. There is nothing wrong with this variety, as long as everyone agrees in advance what the framework of discussion is and how the words are being used.

Similarly, the word 'being' will mean something different in relation to God from what it means in relation to one of his creatures, because the nature of the divine being is different. As long as we know what it is that we are talking about, there is no problem with this, and the word 'being' can be adapted accordingly. But if we say that the word 'being' can only be used of a finite object, then it cannot be applied to God and some other term must be found.

We can see something of this in the analogies which Scripture uses of God. There are times, for example, when he is compared with material objects like fire or rock, or to natural phenomena like the wind. What does it mean to say that 'our God is a consuming fire' (Heb. 12:29), or that he is our 'rock' (Ps. 28:1)? Some people have claimed that descriptions of this kind are survivals of primitive religious beliefs, antedating the more evolved religion of Moses. They say that there was a time when Israel, like other primitive peoples, worshipped fire and natural objects which they believed contained a supernatural power. Perhaps that is true, but it does not explain why, after God revealed himself to the patriarchs as the Lord of heaven and earth, they continued to use such images. There must be something in them which cannot be explained away as the survival of an earlier paganism, especially when they are readily used by the New Testament writers as well.

The answer, of course, is that these terms are not meant to be taken literally, or in every sense of the word. To say that God is a consuming fire means only that he destroys and purifies at the same time, an apparent paradox which is frequently attested in the Old Testament in the context of the Lord's 'visitation', which is always both a blessing and a curse, something which is readily pictured by fire. Similarly, God is not a physical rock, but a spiritual presence which is solid and permanent, in the way that a rock appears to be. We should not forget that the Apostle Peter is also called a rock, on which Jesus will build his church – but whatever that verse means, it cannot mean either that Peter was God or that his bones were ground down to make cement for the foundation of the basilica in Rome which bears his name. One would have to have a singular lack of imagination to think something like that, but unfortunately it sometimes seems that some critics of the Bible are too literalistic for their own good.

When we call God 'Father' we face a similar situation, though perhaps it is somewhat more complicated in that a father is a human person. God's fatherhood is not simply a projection of human fatherhood, which is too broad a concept to fit perfectly. There are many human fathers who are anything but good role models for their children, and we cannot say that God resembles them in any way. There may even be times when this language is unhelpful unless the deep-seated hostility which some people have towards their human fathers can be dealt with first. There is no point in having them transfer their anger onto God. Human fatherhood involves creation, and therefore relationship, but the content of this will vary enormously from case to case, and in some circumstances it may not mean much at all. But divine fatherhood implies a living relationship with God, which is all-important to those who enjoy it. The analogy is partial and selective, but it is possible to define its limits with a fair degree of accuracy. Once again, it is the subject which determines what the parameters are. We know God, and therefore we can say what it is about human fatherhood which fits, and what it is that does not. Once we make that decision, the rest falls neatly into place and there is no real problem any more.

4

'I Am Has Sent Me To You' – The Personal Dimension

The personhood of God

We have now looked fairly comprehensively at the question of God's 'being' and tried to explain why it is necessary to hold on to such a concept. In the process, we have seen that we cannot do this without giving pride of place to our own personal relationship with him. We cannot fathom God's being in the abstract, and what little we know about it has to be mediated through our experience of him in personal terms. This does not invalidate what we have to say about God's being, but it does mean that our knowledge of it is conditioned in important ways which we cannot ignore. But a major part of the argument of the authors of *The Openness of God* is that traditional theology has done just this. According to them, classical theism has preferred an objective description of God which may sound good to a philosopher, but which does not do justice to the subjective considerations which matter most to the ordinary believer. For example, even if it might be true to say that God is 'ineffable' in some way or other, how does that affect my prayer life? If I believe that God is 'wholly other', to use the terminology made famous by Karl Barth (1886–1968), does this mean that I cannot have any meaningful contact with him at all?

These questions are important because, as the authors of *The Openness of God* are quick to point out, the Bible is all about our relationship with God, a phenomenon which it discusses in the most intimate detail. In fact, if that relationship were left out of account, the Bible would not exist, at least not in anything like its present form. All the ups and downs of human experience are found in it, and God is present in the most varied circumstances. This is one of the main reasons why Scripture has such an enduring appeal – it is not, and has never been, an esoteric book of interest only to academic philosophers. But if God is really present and involved in our everyday lives, does this not mean that he must be flexible enough to adapt to our needs as they arise? Can he remain immutable and still deal with us as we are, not as we might be in some ideal philosophical world?

That the God of the Bible is a personal being is so obvious that it hardly needs to be demonstrated. But exactly what that personhood involves is another matter. The ancient Greek gods were personal too, but they were very different from Yahweh. No Greek god, not even Zeus, was the Supreme Being, and when pagan philosophers began to talk of such a Being they did not think of it as personal. That is one of the major differences between any form of Platonism and Christianity, and it raises major questions about the nature and extent of the supposed influence of the former on the latter. However similar the two beliefs may have been in some respects, they differed radically at this point, and that essential difference had immense implications for the way in which their relationship developed.

Modern scholars may think that Christianity was Platonized in the early centuries of the church's existence, but that is not the way it appeared to the Platonists of the time. They continued to believe that Christians had muddied the waters of philosophical purity by imagining that the Supreme Being was personal in character. The notion that this Being was actually three distinct persons, one of whom had become a man, thereby mixing the spiritual (good) with the material (evil), was not just totally unacceptable – it was ludicrous. That the masses of the population, and even the state authorities should get caught up in it was absurd, but the Neoplatonists comforted themselves in their knowledge that philosophical truth had always been the preserve of an élite. The diehards never were won over, and in 529 the Emperor Justinian closed the remaining philosophical schools at

Athens. The survivors emigrated to Persia, unwilling even at that point to come to terms with what to them was the latest insanity.

Christians, for their part, understood the problem which Platonism posed to biblical faith, and they took a completely different line. They insisted both on the goodness of matter, on the ground that it had been created by a God who was good (an insistence which made the incarnation of a good God possible) and also on the resurrection of the flesh. Platonists, if they thought of 'salvation' at all, conceived of it as the liberation of the divine soul, which had got itself imprisoned in a material body, but this went completely against Christian teaching and the church refused to give in. These were the most important issues, but there were dozens of others where the early Christians took a stand against the prevailing wisdom of their age. In the end they completely rejected the world-view of the ancient Greeks, and even those who spoke Greek ceased to think of themselves as 'Hellenes'.[19] Rejection of the pagan past could hardly have gone any farther than that.

The inadequacy of ancient philosophy to provide a framework for the construction of Christian theology is nowhere more evident than in its failure to produce a term which could adequately express the concept of personhood. The biblical God's personhood could hardly be more obvious, so much so that it appears to have been taken for granted by the Israelites who did not have a word for it either, although there were plenty of other ways in which they could (and did) express the same idea. In the Old Testament this was done primarily through the concept of the 'name', which carried with it overtones of personal presence and authority which we find hard to imagine today. In the modern world, names are really only convenient labels for identifying people. They can be changed or added to without any real problem. The fact that my name means 'strong warrior' is of no significance to me or to anybody else. But in the Bible it is very

---

[19] This word meant 'pagan' and was avoided by the Greeks themselves until the creation of a Greek state in the early nineteenth century. Before that time, they called themselves 'Romans', or even just 'Christians'.

different. People were given names not merely in order to distinguish them from others, but in order to say something about their character and destiny. The most famous case is that of Jesus, who was given that name precisely because he would save his people from their sins, and 'Jesus' (or 'Joshua', from the Hebrew *Yehoshua*) means 'God has saved'. Such names were used with reverence and treated as meaningful by those who used them. Sometimes they could even acquire new meanings, as when Cephas (Peter) became the 'rock' on which the future church would be built. That cannot have been what his parents intended when they originally gave him that name!

God's own personal name *YHWH* was regarded with such awe in ancient times that it was never pronounced. Instead, the Jews substituted other words when they had to refer to it. Most commonly they replaced it by *Adonai* ('my Lord') and this habit was carried over into the Greek translation made about 200 BC, which we call the Septuagint.[20] From there it passed into the New Testament and Christian usage generally, so that we no longer hear or see the name *YHWH* at all. Occasionally we come across the form 'Jehovah', which is a Latinized version of the Hebrew consonants plus the vowels of *Adonai* – a hybrid form which was never used by anybody in ancient times, in spite of what modern Jehovah's Witnesses claim. The personal name of God was treated in this way out of respect for who God is. The Jews were fully aware that they had been given knowledge of a being who is beyond human understanding, and their veiling of the divine name is a sign of this. As with the pattern of the temple and many other things in Old Testament religion, it is a picture of how God dwelt among them and yet was hidden from them.

But although God's name was hidden in this way, it was certainly not ignored. On the contrary, the Old Testament is full of examples where the name of God is appealed to as the basis for his merciful intervention in the affairs of Israel. Of course this

---

[20] When vowel markings were added to the Hebrew Bible (sometime after AD 500) the name *YHWH* was left unpointed as a reminder that another word would have to be substituted for it.

was not a magical appeal to four Hebrew letters, but a conscious and rational reliance on the meaning which those letters convey. The name of God is powerful because God is the supreme being, the absolute I AM, against whom no other power can prevail. Furthermore, by revealing his name to Israel, God was tying his reputation to theirs, as the psalmists and prophets were never slow to point out. This meant that God would not abandon them or allow them to be exterminated, as so many other ancient peoples and empires were, but it also laid special obligations on the Israelites. For them to insult or abuse the name of God was to blaspheme him personally, and this was strictly forbidden by the third commandment (Ex. 20:7). Everything connected with God's holiness and power resided in his name, which was the basis of the covenant relationship which he established and maintained with his people.

When we come to the New Testament however, this pattern alters. When the disciples asked Jesus how they should pray, Jesus told them to say 'Our Father'. This was not a form of address to God which had any currency in Israel, and Jesus caused consternation among the Jews when he used it (see John 5:18). It was so typical of him that later on the Apostle Paul used the Aramaic word *Abba*, which Jesus would have used, when he described to the Galatians how the Holy Spirit helps us to pray (Gal. 4:6). It seems that even the disciples did not really understand the significance of this, because at one point Philip asked Jesus to show them the Father (John 14:8). Would he have done that if he had identified the Father with the invisible *YHWH*? We are not surprised that Jesus rebuked him for asking such a thing, but from the Jewish point of view his reply is disconcerting, to say the least. Far from telling Philip the 'obvious', namely that the Father, being *YHWH*, is invisible and cannot be seen, he says more or less the exact opposite – 'if you have seen me, you have seen the Father' (John 14:9).

This claim, and the intimacy with God which it implies, raises serious questions for our understanding of God's personhood. It is quite clear from everything else that Jesus says that the Father is God, and so when he says that he and the Father indwell each other to such an extent that to see one is to see the other, Jesus is in effect claiming to be God himself. But if Jesus and the Father are the same, and there is only one God, how can there be any distinction between the Father and the Son? Must it not therefore be the case that what is presented to us as two separate 'persons' is in fact but a single divine reality which we perceive in different ways?

This was the logic behind modalism, according to which the persons of the Godhead are merely modes of God's self-revelation in the world. Modalism is a constant temptation for any philosophical theology because it emphasizes the oneness of the divine being and finds any notion of plurality in it uncongenial. After having been defeated in ancient times, it made a comeback in the later seventeenth century when the doctrine of the trinity fell into disfavour and many theologians became unitarians. There was even a Unitarian Church set up, which had a number of influential spokesmen in the nineteenth century and which continues to exist today. But the influence of unitarian ideas has extended far beyond the confines of the church which goes by that name. Even such a great defender of trinitarian doctrine as Karl Barth has been accused of modalism, and not without some justification. Barth disliked the term 'person' and preferred to speak of Father, Son and Holy Spirit as 'modes of being' (*Seinsweise*) which cannot fail to evoke the essentially unitarian climate in which he was brought up.

The doctrine of the trinity continues to cause serious problems for many people, even though interest in it has enjoyed a renaissance in recent years. The evidence of John's Gospel certainly makes it clear that the Father and the Son are separate persons, because however closely identified they may be, they nevertheless communicate with each other in a way which implies personal interaction. In the great 'high priestly' prayer of Jesus in John 17 this is made quite explicit – nobody would suggest that Jesus was just talking to himself. How it is possible for Jesus to be God when there is only one God was the main theme of the Christological debates of the fourth century, which resulted in the doctrinal statement that we now call the Nicene Creed.

Initially, most people tried to resolve the problem by focussing on the biblical statement that the Son is the 'only-begotten' of the Father (John 1:14), and interpreting this to mean that while the Father is basically God (and identical to *YHWH*), he at some point produced a Son who was just like him. But at what point? This was the issue raised by Arius, who assumed that birth could only take place in time, and that therefore there must have been a time before the Son existed. But this was ruled out by the fact that God is eternal, so time concepts have no meaning when speaking about him. However we interpret the begotten-ness of the Son, it must be understood in the context of eternity, which is why the creed speaks of him as 'eternally begotten' – a logical contradiction if you stop to think about it, but a necessary affirmation if we want to do justice to the teaching of Scripture.

This idea was later extended to cover the Holy Spirit, who proceeds from the Father (John 15:26). The personhood of the Holy Spirit is less obvious than that of the Son because he is in effect anonymous. Both the Father and the Son are holy, and both are 'spirit', so neither of these words can be regarded as unique to the Third Person. This peculiarity has been explained by saying that the Holy Spirit's anonymity is due to the fact that it is his task to point us to the Father and the Son, not to himself. But although this is certainly true, it is hard to see why the Holy Spirit has to be anonymous in order to do that. In the end we just have to accept that it is so, without looking for reasons which can only be speculation rather than fact. But it is quite clear from a number of New Testament passages that he is both personal and divine, and so he must be ranked with the Father and the Son, even if his name is not precisely analogous to theirs. The New Testament evidence was brought together by Basil of Caesarea (*c.* 329–79) in his famous book on the Holy Spirit, which provided the basis for the third article of the Nicene Creed. This tells us that the Spirit is 'the Lord, the giver of life, who proceeds from the Father . . .'[21]

---

[21] Western versions add here 'and the Son', but this was not in the original version and is controversial (to say the least) in ecumenical dialogue between the Eastern (Orthodox) and Western (Catholic and Protestant) churches.

With the Father and the Son he is worshipped and glorified. He has spoken through the prophets.' Add it all up, said Basil, and you have another divine person, making the trinity as we find it in the creed.

Basil's work was of capital importance, but there are certain respects in which it can be said that it was not fully adequate to meet the challenge of defining the biblical doctrine of the three persons in God. One of the difficulties with Basil's approach is that it led to a picture of the trinity in which the Father was the 'cause' of the other two persons. This did not strike his contemporaries as problematic because it was assumed that the Father could be equated with *YHWH*. But the New Testament tells us that the Son was present at the creation of the world, and that he must be regarded as the creator every bit as much as the Father is (John 1:3; Col. 1:16), which makes the Father = *YHWH* equation less obvious than it might otherwise seem. The truth is that, in Christ, our relationship with God has changed, and it is not helpful to think of *YHWH* as only one of the persons of the trinity. As we have already seen, when we want to compare the Old Testament revelation of God with the New Testament one, it is better to think in terms of 'outside' and 'inside', i.e. the same God perceived in a different way, than to think of a pre-existing Father who in some incomprehensible way 'gave birth' to a Son and 'sent out' the Holy Spirit.

Once we do this, we realize that the personal names of the trinity are identifiers to help us understand how they relate to one another and to us, not statements of where they originally came from. This was clearly understood by Augustine (354–430), whose great work on the trinity remains the standard treatment of the subject as far as classical Western theism is concerned.[22] Augustine stressed that the important thing about the persons of the trinity was the structure of the relations which they enjoyed with one another, and that these relations could be most clearly

---

[22] This is an important qualifier. Augustine's work was not translated into Greek until the late thirteenth century, and it has never enjoyed the prominence in Eastern Christianity which it has in the West.

understood in terms of love. For God to be love, said Augustine, there had to be someone to do the loving, someone to be loved, and love itself. He therefore argued that the Father is the Lover, the Son is the Beloved and the Holy Spirit is the Love who flows between them (in both directions – proceeding from the Father initially but also from the Son, who responds to the Father's love with an equal love of his own).

It is possible to quarrel with this presentation of the matter, particularly because of the way in which it subtly depersonalizes the Holy Spirit, and it would be wrong to suggest that Augustine has had the last word on the subject of the trinity. Nevertheless, his basic intuition about the importance of the relations for our understanding of the persons is surely correct. It is as they relate to each other that the perfection of the divine love is realized, and it is against this that our experience of that love must be measured. This is particularly important when we consider Christ's atoning work on the cross. We often think and preach that 'Christ died for me', but this can be a highly misleading statement if it is taken out of its wider theological context. It is certainly not true to talk as if there was some kind of agreement between him and us, according to which he agreed to pay the price for my sins in return for my faith and obedience to him.

The key to understanding Jesus' death for me is to remember that at a more fundamental level he was doing his Father's will. In other words, he was dying in the first instance *for the Father's sake*, because it was the Father's will that the Son should die for those sinners whom he wished to redeem. We cannot appreciate the atonement unless we give pride of place to the relationship between the Father and the Son – a point which is stressed over and over again in the Gospels. When we are saved in Christ, we are taken into that relationship by the Holy Spirit, who enables us to have fellowship with them. This is quite clearly stated by the Apostle Paul in Galatians 4:6: 'Because you are sons, God sent the Spirit of his Son into our hearts, the Spirit who calls out "*Abba*, Father".'

In Christ we have been adopted as sons, and therefore we have the privilege of addressing the Father in the same terms as those used by the Son. The agent of our prayers is the Holy Spirit who, because he comes from the Son, has the authority to give us this privilege. The doctrine of the trinity is not a complex philosophical theory which is just an added extra to our faith. On the contrary, it is the one coherent explanation of Christian experience, the ultimate foundation of our prayer life. We cannot function as Christians without it.

A further point which we might mention here concerns the so-called 'masculinity' of God. This was not a problem for many centuries, but in recent years it has been called into question by the feminist movement. Is God male? Of course, in one sense he is not, and masculine imagery used of him is analogical in much the same way as other images in Scripture are. But in another way he is, because in Christ the Son became a man, not a woman. Furthermore, we are told by the Apostle Paul that Adam was created in the image of God, but that Eve was created in the image of Adam (1 Cor 11:7). She therefore shares the image of God at one remove, through him. This is not a popular notion with feminists, but it is difficult to see how the God of the Bible can be perceived in any other way. Those who try to neuter him, or who want to replace words like Father and Son with Parent and Child are not being faithful to the biblical witness. Does this mean that male human beings are somehow better off than females? Of course not. We have to remember that the church is portrayed as the bride of Christ, so that in relation to him there is a sense in which we are all 'female'. The headship of the male is given to us as a sign of God's sovereignty, but it does not imply domination. On the contrary, it means sacrifice, because Christ gave himself up for the benefit of his bride, as the Apostle Paul pointed out (Eph. 5:22–33). God's masculinity is more than just an analogy, but it cannot be assimilated to some kind of patriarchal human pattern. It has to be understood in the overall context of our relationship with him and interpreted accordingly. When we do this, our human understandings are transformed by the divine presence in our lives, and what appears to be unfair becomes instead the only real basis on which healthy human relationships can develop.

Relating to God

Given that the trinity is the context in which we are called into a relationship with God, can we find a coherent linguistic framework in which to express it? The authors of *The Openness of God* are right to suggest that philosophical categories are not very helpful in doing this. This is not because they are invalid, but because the context is different. The word 'person' does not come from philosophy, as we have already demonstrated, and does not fit comfortably in that sort of framework, as the persistence of modalism indicates. We need to look elsewhere for the right model.

Fortunately, the Bible itself provides a model: law, which is a rational discipline requiring a high degree of logical expertise, but which at the same time deals with reality in a practical and not an abstract manner. As a result, it is capable of combining differing perspectives which to the philosophical mind appear to be anomalies. A very good example of how this works can be seen in the British system of government. On paper, Britain is a monarchy where everybody does the queen's will. Parliament appears on the surface to be no more than an advisory body, and in fact it is possible for the sovereign to reject a piece of legislation by saying '*La reine s'avisera*', which literally means 'The queen will advise herself'. Of course everybody knows that this is not the case at all, and that the British system of government is really very different from what appears on the surface. Every once in a while people come along who suggest that it ought to be rationalized by establishing a visibly democratic régime in which the form and the substance coincide. They do not usually want to change the substance much; what worries them is the form in which it is presented (or concealed).

People who say things like this do not get their way because the 'problem' which they have discovered is a false one. It worries theorists but does not trouble lawyers at all. Everybody knows what the queen can and cannot do, and the fact that this is not immediately apparent in the law does not change matters in the slightest. In fact, it allows for flexibility in extraordinary circumstances which cannot be foreseen, and provides as much assurance as anything can that no unsuitable person will usurp supreme power in the state. The theorists can grumble all they like about archaic privilege and so on, but practical people carry on in the knowledge that this is really irrelevant to the workings of government, which might well turn out to be less satisfactory if they were 'rationalized' as the theorists want.

This ability of the law to embrace theoretical contradictions makes it a more suitable vehicle than philosophy for defining the relationship which we have with God, and it is probably for this reason that it is the way of thinking which the Bible actually uses. According to the Scriptures, the Christian church is governed by a covenant. This covenant is not originally Christian – as we have already seen, it goes back to Abraham, and in some sense it still embraces the Jewish people (Rom. 9–11). It is personal, because it was established with him and with his descendants, particularly with his son Isaac and his grandson Jacob. But Jacob was given the name Israel, and so became the eponymous founder of the covenant nation. This means that the covenant is both individual and collective at the same time – another apparent anomaly which has provided grist for more than one theological mill. In the twentieth century it has been fashionable to talk about 'corporate personality', an idea which takes the emphasis off the necessity of individual salvation and puts it on the election of the collective body of the church instead. In practical terms, this may mean that it is not necessary to ask whether or not I am saved as an individual, because as long as I belong to the church, I can hope to share in a common salvation.

The truth of course, is that both things are important, and that to turn the individual/corporate contrast into an either/or choice is a mistake. As we have just seen, Israel is primarily the name of an individual – it was given to Jacob because he wrestled with the angel of God and prevailed (Gen. 32:28). From there it passed to all Jacob's descendants who have inherited his legacy and are defined by it. What this means is that everyone who belongs to this family is expected to imitate Jacob in his relationship with God. This is a responsibility placed on each individual Israelite, as the Apostle Paul pointed out, taking this right back to Abraham (Rom. 4:16–17). Of course, not all Israelites accepted this responsibility, but in that case they were not really members of the family or heirs to the covenant, whatever they might claim to the contrary. On the other hand, those who subscribed to the covenant could be integrated into the national family ('naturalized' as we would say in a secular context) and become inheritors of the promises. Because of its legal character, the covenant could stretch beyond the blood tie. The main argument of Paul's letter to the Romans is that those who had no entitlement by nature could receive it by grace, which is the basis of our standing before God.

Within the covenant framework we can cope with a number of different situations which may otherwise be irreconcilable. Can I be a child of the covenant without being saved? Yes. This was certainly true of large numbers in Israel, and we can say the same for many members of the visible church today. We certainly cannot say for sure that everyone sitting around us in the pews is going to be with us in heaven. From another perspective, does being a member of the church excuse me from having to have a personal relationship with God? No. This is required of us all, for the simple reason that we have one already by virtue of our creation. The issue is not whether to have a relationship or not; it is whether the relationship which we have is right or wrong.

This is a key point which is not always fully understood. There is no human being who does not have a relationship with God, because each one of us has been created in his image and likeness (Gen. 1:26–27). This point is reinforced by the Apostle Paul, who tells us that, because of this, everyone is responsible for sin, whether this has been specifically pointed out or not (Rom. 1:18–20). Ignorance of the law is no excuse. By virtue of our birth we are in a relationship with God, and it is invariably the wrong one, because it is the relationship which we have inherited from Adam – disobedience and rebellion. By being born again in Christ, this wrong relationship is put right and we enter into the fellowship with God which Adam was presumably meant to enjoy and which was fully realized in Jesus. As he is the natural Son of God, so we are sons and daughters by adoption, sharing in the rights and privileges of the divine family without partaking of the same essential being.

In terms of everyday living, the greatest privilege which we have as God's children is the right to approach him in prayer. This is all-important, because it gives us access to his sovereign will and power in a way which would not otherwise be possible. There can be no more wonderful blessing than the fact that God is prepared to listen to our prayers – nothing we need is too small or too unimportant for him to be concerned about. Jesus taught his disciples this in the Sermon on the Mount. He told them to look at the birds and flowers and then consider that the same God who takes care of them takes care of us as well (Matt. 6:26–32). Because of this, Jesus went on to tell them not to be preoccupied with the necessities of everyday life. Rather than worry unduly about things which God would provide anyway, it would be better for them to concentrate on the things which really matter – righteousness and the kingdom of God.

This advice to the disciples gives us a pattern for our prayer lives as well. We all tend to think in selfish terms when we pray, and look at God as someone whose primary concern is to supply our personal wants – whether they are genuine needs or not. Sad to say, there are many people who treat God as if he were a kind of vending machine. They put their prayer in the right slot, push the button and expect the answer to be delivered automatically. If that does not happen, they kick the machine and go off to try something else. It hardly seems necessary to say that an attitude like that is the very opposite of the true spirit of intercessory prayer, and if that is the way we behave, then we should not be surprised if God ignores us. Before he starts to hear our prayers and answer them, he has to teach us to approach him in the right way, and with the right attitude. If we fail in that, we shall inevitably fail in everything which depends on it as well.

Once we have the right approach to God and the right attitude towards him, the next thing we have to remember is that God knows what our needs are even before we ask him. In fact he knows them much better than we do. This is not surprising, since any parent knows what a child needs, even if it is not at all what the child wants or is asking for. A major part of bringing up children, after all, is teaching them what their real needs and their true interests are. Many an unfulfilled request is for the child's own good, though it will not seem like that to the child. This is the way we have to understand our relationship to God. He is our Father and we are his children, who have to learn by experience what is right and what is wrong for us. The way in which God answers prayer is one of the most effective and instructive learning tools which the Christian has.

God's purpose for us as his children is that we should become holy, in order that we may be prepared to live with him in eternity. This does not mean that there is not a great deal of flexibility and variety in the Christian life. The Apostle John told people that he would not die in the same way as Peter because that was what Jesus wanted and it was not for them to decide otherwise (John 21:20–23). So it often is with us. One person gets one thing and another another because that is the way that God has planned it. There is no room for jealously here; we are each called to live our own life in the sight of God. Perhaps the best image to describe this is that of a teacher with a class full of pupils. The lesson is the same, and the learning goals are identical, but each pupil will have his or her own special approach and difficulties, which a good teacher will recognize and adapt to. In some cases it may mean that one or two pupils are given a great deal more attention than the majority, while a few may not need (or get) much at all. Does this mean that the teacher is capricious and untrustworthy, or that he plays favourites? Of course not. It means only that he takes care of each pupil individually, according to the way that is right and best for them. So it is in our relationship with God.

Of course we have to remember that this individual care and attention must be balanced against the needs of the community. Let us say that I have been given a gift like speaking in tongues, which it is right for me to have at that particular moment. What should I do with this gift? The Apostle Paul had to face this issue in the Corinthian church because people were evidently pressing their own claims to have various gifts at the expense of the overall harmony of the congregation. Paul told them that they were to use their gifts in a way which contributed to the building up of the church, and if that meant keeping quiet, then they were to keep quiet (1 Cor. 14:28).

The normal pattern is that God works through individuals for the benefit of the community, to which we are all called to contribute. If our prayer requests do not fit into that pattern, they are unlikely to get a positive answer, because that is not what God wants for us. This does not mean that we should never pray for things which we need for ourselves, but that we should understand how and why God gives them to (or withholds them from) us. In my own experience, for example, I prayed for many years that I might have more time to teach and study the things that I was trained to do, instead of being immersed in a sea of administrative duties, and God heard my prayer. In fact it was answered in the most wonderful way – eventually. But before I understood what the answer was, I had to suffer some very different things, including the loss of my job and even exile.

This kind of story is by no means unique, and many Christians can share similar experiences in their own lives. Others may go through quite different trials and temptations because God is dealing differently with them. The common factor in all of this is that it is the same God at work, achieving the same overall purpose for all of us. The way itself may be different, but the goal is the same and the God who takes us there is the same too. It is what the psalmist discovered so many years ago:

> For his anger lasts only a moment, but his favour lasts a lifetime;
> Weeping may remain for a night, but rejoicing comes in the morning.
>   (Ps. 30:5)

When Christ who is our light appears, the tears and sorrows of our present darkness will pass away, and we shall rejoice with all the saints in that peace of God which passes understanding.

Can my prayers change God's mind? Sometimes the Bible seems to suggest that they can, and certainly intercessory prayer must have some function. It is hard to believe that God would have commanded us to bring our requests to him if there were no point in asking him for anything to begin with. The Bible not infrequently says that God 'repented' of some evil or other which he was going to inflict because of the prayers of his faithful people, so there must surely be something in this idea. But what?

To try to understand this, we must start with the covenant context in which our relationship with God is worked out. We are seated with Christ in the heavenly places (Eph. 2:6) and it is the Holy Spirit who teaches us how to pray (Gal. 4:6). Therefore, if our relationship with God is right, what we pray will be inspired by him. Because it is the Holy Spirit who teaches us how to pray and who, in doing so, conforms us to the image of the Son, there is a sense in which we might even say that God is hearing and answering his own prayers. More precisely, we can say that the Father is answering prayers which have been inspired by the Spirit according to the will of the Son. If that is the case, then God's so-called 'changes of heart' are not the result of external pressure applied by us, but are the fruit of an inner dialogue among the persons of the trinity, in which we are privileged to participate by grace. Does this mean that God changes as he hears our prayers? Not at all. We are the ones who are being changed, because in all this mysterious process we are being drawn more deeply into fellowship with God, and into an understanding of his will. Intercessory prayer is his way of doing this, and we should not be surprised to discover that very often the way it works appears to be every bit as convoluted as we are. God knows who he is dealing with, after all!

Becoming like God

The ultimate goal of the Christian life is that we should become like God. How is this possible? We cannot become like his unfathomable being, because in that respect he will always be totally different from us. An adopted child can perhaps acquire many of his adopted parents' characteristics, but he cannot become their flesh and blood, and so it is with us in our relationship to God. Our likeness to him is not a natural one, but the gift of his grace, and so it must be sought in a way and at a level which makes sense for us. There are two ways in which we are like God, or can become like him, and we shall look at each one in turn.

First, there is the fact that we have been created in his image and likeness (Gen. 1:26–27). This makes us like God in a way which sets us apart from all other creatures. I often make this point to my students by telling them that if a dog were to bite their leg, it would be painful, but they would probably not do much to the dog or blame him seriously for what he had done. But if I were to bite their leg, it would be a very different story. The pain would probably be a good deal less, since my teeth are far less sharp than most dogs' teeth, but that is hardly the point. It is not the degree of injury which matters, but the responsibility which may legitimately be attributed to the agent who caused it. In the second case, I would be responsible, and therefore guilty, because I should have known better, and should have respected the fact that both I and the other person are creatures made in God's image. In this respect, it is important to note that references to God's image in us which occur in the Bible *after* the fall of Adam are frequently concerned with just this kind of thing. We are told that we are not to kill other people because, like us, they were made in God's image (Gen. 9:5–6). We are not even to insult them, for the same reason (James 3:9). In terms of the divine image, we have an inbuilt resemblance to God, and it is our duty as human beings to behave accordingly.

But there is another way in which we are not yet like God, and becoming like him in this way is what the Christian life is all about. We are not yet holy as God is holy, but we are called to become so, and the Bible is our guide as to how to get there (Lev. 20:7–8; 1 Thess. 4:3). Holiness is a word which has acquired a somewhat dubious reputation because of the way in which it has frequently been misunderstood. There is a persistent tradition in the church, going back to ancient times, which regards holiness as essentially a matter of abstinence. We are not to smoke, not to drink, not to marry, not to . . . The list is seemingly endless. Such prohibitions, however beneficial they may be in themselves, miss the point because they refer to external habits rather than to the inward disposition of heart and mind which ought to govern all our behaviour. It is the latter which counts, and which determines whether or not we are achieving the goal which God has set for us.

Holiness is not an option for the Christian – it is a necessity because without it we cannot approach God or have fellowship with him. Outwardly it may lead to many different forms of self-discipline – devotional exercises such as daily Bible reading and prayer, listening to the preaching of God's Word, participation in the sacraments, and so on. Abstinence of various kinds may also have an important part to play in this, since the Bible tells us to fast and to refrain from sexual intercourse at different times. But none of these things *by themselves* is enough – or anything like enough – to get us closer to God or to make us holy. It is only the inner disposition of our hearts which will achieve that, as we rely on God and trust him to fill us with his grace. This disposition is not something we can work up or wish on ourselves – it is a gift of the Holy Spirit, who dwells in our hearts by faith. We are sanctified by faith, not by works, however important the latter may be in their proper place, because faith is the gift of God's presence and power to us.

Perhaps we can best summarize all this by asking ourselves three short questions. Does God understand me and what I am like? Yes. Does God accept me as I am, with all my faults and shortcomings? Yes. Does God leave me where he found me? No. It is not God who changes to suit me, but I who am changed to suit him. This difference is all-important, and understanding it is the true key to the Christian life.

The openness of God

And so we return to where we started. The authors of *The Openness of God* were concerned that we should not have a picture of God which would make it impossible for him to be responsive to our prayers. They believed that traditional theology had created such a picture, and that in order to be faithful to the teaching of the Bible theology would have to be reconstructed along much more flexible lines. Their intentions were good, and their main concern is one which all of us must share. Nobody wants to see people cut off from God by an inadequate theology. Unfortunately, however, the realization of these intentions was not helped by the fact that these authors confused their categories of thought. They supposed that God's infinite flexibility in dealing with us must indicate that his being is somehow changeable. It did not seem to occur to them that it might be possible for the creator to relate to his creatures without changing, or that such a relationship is essential if we are ever going to trust God, or become the people that he wants us to be.

At a deeper level, it seems that the authors of *The Openness of God* have not reckoned with the seriousness of human sin. It is because of our sin that we are not what we should be, and that God's work of salvation in Christ was necessary. It is because of our sin that the Christian life takes the shape that it does, with all its ups and downs, as we strive to attain the holiness which is our inheritance in Christ. Finally, it is because of our sin that we have to be changed into creatures who are pleasing to God and fit to stand in his presence. God has not sinned, and so none of this applies to him. He cannot change, because even if he does something which might look to us like 'change' he would still be the same as he was before – the ultimate and absolute ruler of the universe. A word like 'change' simply makes no sense when it is applied to God. Classical theism is not perfect, and it does not have the answer to every question. But fifty generations of Christians have not been wrong to insist on the basic principles which that traditional theology has sought to uphold. God is who he is – the ever-living, all-powerful Sovereign Lord who is our Saviour and our Redeemer. In the end we are brought back to the words of the psalmist, which were quoted centuries later by the writer of the Epistle to the Hebrews, and which still apply today:

> In the beginning you laid the foundations of the earth, and the heavens are the work of your hands.
> They will perish, but you remain; they will all wear out like a garment.
> Like clothing you will change them and they will be discarded.
> But you remain the same and your years will never end.
>
> (Ps. 102: 25–27; Heb. 1:10–12)

Amen.

Index